PASTORAL LEADERSHIP AND CHURCH GOVERNMENT

Study Guide for Pastors, Ministers, and Deacons on Church Government

For the New Testament Church

2nd Edition

BISHOP HARRY L. HERMAN, D.D., TH.D.

EDITOR-IN-CHIEF
Elder Eric A. Beda, MBA

Copyright © 1997, 2016 by Alpha Omega Publishing Company
All rights reserved.
No part of this document may be reproduced or transmitted in any form or by any means, electronic, mechanical, photocopying, or recording without prior written permission from Alpha Omega Publishing, except in the case of brief quotations embedded in critical articles and reviews.

Published in the United States by
Alpha Omega Publishing Company
P.O. Box 353, Jackson, MI 49204
Library of Congress Control Number: 2017931855
ISBN: 978-0-9985799-0-0

Adapted from *Church Government: A Study Guide of Pastoral Administration* © 1997 by Harry L. Herman, D.D., Th.D.

All scripture quotations are derived from the Holy Bible, *King James Version*.

Herman, Harry L.
1. Pastoral Leadership. 2. Church Governing Authority 3. Confession and Restoration. 4. Tithes and Offerings 5. Role of Deacons/Church Board

Alpha Omega Publishing Company publishes books that promote the discussion and understanding of the Pentecostal movement throughout the four corners of the world since the Day of Pentecost. These books are made possible by the enthusiasm of our readers; the support of a committed group of donors, large and small; the collaboration of our many partners in the independent media and ecclesiastical organizations; booksellers, who often hand-sell Alpha Omega Publishing books; librarians; and above all by our authors.
Books may be purchased in quantity and/or special sales by contacting the publisher:

Alpha Omega Publishing
P: 517-879-1286
E: info@omegapublishing.org
www.omegapublishing.org
Printed in the United States of America

There are three individuals that have effectuated my ministry, the teaching of Bishop R.P. Paddock, the leadership of Bishop Herman, and the preaching of Bishop David Lee Ellis.

-- **Bishop Combs, MI**

In reading and studying on the first five pages of the book I've learned that God had set in motion how we are to be governed. The principle of "headship" and rule was established in the Garden. The husband is the head over the wife as Jesus is the head of the church.

-- **Janell, MI**

My beliefs were confirmed that God chooses the Pastors. The number one thing that he/she must do is govern and instruct the people; doing so from God's voice and watching carefully for their souls.

-- **Robert, GA**

Reading the words on a piece of paper is one thing, but understanding the depth of their meaning is another. I have always known the teachings of Bishop Paddock and Bishop Herman, as I have sat in their classes. But it wasn't until today that it hit home, and my understanding and revelation of what they were teaching came alive for me after reviewing this book.

--**Carol, MI**

After being saved for over 30 years, it is a blessing to get a more in-depth understanding of scripture.

--**Regina, MI**

Thank you for this book. This book has challenged me to do a thorough study of the word of God.

-- **Brenda, AL**

Table of Contents

Preface
vii

Acknowledgement
viii

Introduction
xi

1. The Church
1

2. The Pastor
7

3. Church Membership
19

4. Church Rule
29

5. Role of Deacons
33

6. Judgment In The Church
37

7. Confession And Restoration
55

8. Tithes and Offerings
71

Afterword
97

Author
99

Preface

This book is written for pastors who want to serve God wholeheartedly according to the right division of the scriptures. It is written to admonish pastors and church leaders on how to effectively manage the flock that the Holy Ghost has made them overseers. Be shepherds of the church of God, which He bought with his own blood. It provides pastors a platform and a blueprint to govern God's church. It is my hope and prayer that this book equips and empowers you to care for the flock that God has entrusted to you and willingly watch over it, not grudgingly nor for what you will get out of it, but because you are eager to serve God. Last, but definitely not least, I am writing this book to remind pastors and ministers, do not serve as lord over the people assigned to your care, but lead them by your own good example. After you have done well, when the Great Shepherd appears, you will receive a crown of glory and honor.

Acknowledgement

This book is dedicated to the memory of the late Bishop Ross Perry Paddock who worked so diligently in the Northern District Council, the Pentecostal Assemblies of the World, and the Apostolic World Christian Fellowship at large. His teachings will long be remembered as the foundation for the administration of many of our present day churches. His vision and revelation of the Word of God has been an inspiration for numerous pastors. "Church Government" was an important subject for Bishop Paddock and it is my privilege to have a part in continuing this outstanding legacy.

I want to express sincere thanks to my wife and God-given helpmeet, Dr. "Jerry" for her willing help in all phases of putting the original book together. Her editing skills were an invaluable asset in compiling the contents of this publication by proofreading each page, correcting common spelling errors and ensuring the use of proper grammar. Her assistance in collating and binding the printed pages into a single book was very much appreciated. For without her help, the work would have been more difficult.

Finally, I would like to thank the many District Elders, Pastors, Ministers and local Church Members of the Northern District Council who have supported me by attending the several seminars taught throughout the State of Michigan. I also appreciate the many positive comments as a result of the material presented at these conferences. Knowledge is a powerful thing; the more we know and learn, the more competent we become and helpful to the people we teach.

Introduction

A government is a system of rule by which a group of people is directed to conduct their affairs in an organized manner under the authority of central leadership. One function of government is to provide a system for the many to cooperate as a single unit for the benefit of the whole. One of the most devastating times in Israel's history was when each man "did that which was right in <u>his</u> own eyes" *(Judges 21:25)*. For any group or individual to function independently without some form of unifying rule is anarchy and results in chaos. At no time are we free to do our own thing. All of us are under some level of government, be it in the home, an organization, the workplace, our local community, state, or country. There are rules that govern our conducts, freedoms, responsibilities, obligations, and privileges regardless of where we reside.

INTRODUCTION

In short, government is a way of life for us all. There is no way it can be circumvented. Why is it so? Simply because God, who is the author of all authority, has determined that creation be subject to the governing forces of His will and purpose. From the beginning of time, God established a system of rule for Lucifer who was the "anointed cherub that covereth" the Arch Angel that had rule over the others *(Ezekiel 28:11-19; Isaiah 14:12-17)*. In the Garden of Eden God established a single rule for Adam to follow and when there were just two (Adam and Eve), Eve became subject to her husband thus providing a system of rule for the smallest unit of society--the family.

Government and organization have always been a priority with God and His people. When the sons of Jacob grew into a nation, they were divided into tribes. Each tribe had a head and was organized in multiple levels of authority. Though they acted independently, they were first under the central authority of Moses, then Joshua and finally Judges who judged the people. In every case, there were central leaders and sub-leaders. In a similar manner, the local church is an independent entity under the leadership of a pastor, and all local churches combined are subject to their head, the Chief Shepherd, Jesus Christ. When the time of the Kings came on the scene, with Saul as Israel's first king, a political central government was established. Under King David, the Levites were organized into 24 courses all subject to the High Priest in the service of the temple.

When Jesus set us free, he did not release us from being governed. To the contrary, He, through systems already established, placed us under a stricter rule than in the past. Let us begin the subject of Church

Government, <u>the</u> system of authority that governs those in the Body of Christ.

This study of Pastoral Leadership and Church Governance is divided into four sections, each one equally important:

Governing procedures: rulers and authority established in the church.

Judgment for violation of God's law, excommunication & disciplinary action.

Confession and restoration: the process of being reconciled with God.

Financial support of the church: tithes and offerings.

Also, let us keep in mind what the functions of the church are:

It is the place of salvation and reconciliation with Jesus Christ.

It is a bread house, the place where souls are fed.

It is a schoolhouse where souls are spiritually educated.

It is a courthouse where transgressors are judged and "rehabilitated."

1
The Church

1. What is it?
2. Whose is it?
3. How was it established?
4. What is its authority?
5. Who is its head?

The church is described by different descriptive words depending on the particular relationship it has with Christ.

- It is referred to as a *BUILDING*, Jesus Christ the foundation and builder *(Psalms 118:22; Matthew 21:42; Act 4:11)*.
- It is called *THE BODY OF CHRIST*, with Jesus Christ as the head *(1 Corinthians 12:27)*.

- It is called the *FLOCK OF GOD,* with Jesus Christ the Chief Shepherd *(1 Peter 5:2-4).*
- It is referred to as the *BRIDE OF CHRIST*, with Jesus Christ the bridegroom *(Revelation 21:9).*

Jesus said, *"and I say unto thee, Thou art Peter, and upon this rock, I will build my church, and the gates of hell shall not prevail against it"* (Matthew 16:18).

The Foundation

Every building needs a foundation if it is to survive the test that will come against it. The New Testament church has for its foundation the *Revelation of Who Jesus is!* Peter has just stated that Jesus was the Christ (the Messiah) the Son of the Living God *(Matthew 16:16-17)*, and it was this "revelation" that is the foundation of the church. It is not a little boy sent by the father, but Elohim Himself whom Isaiah prophesied was to come in Isaiah 9:6 who was the long awaited Messiah. This Christ is Emmanuel, *"God with us" (Matthew 1:23)*; the invisible Creator who took on the mantle of flesh through the womb of Mary. Only the Almighty God would be strong and enduring enough to lay in Zion a foundation for His church. *"Therefore thus saith the Lord GOD, Behold, I lay in Zion for a foundation a stone a tried stone, a precious cornerstone, a sure foundation: he that believeth shall not make haste" (Isaiah 28:16).* Peter is NOT the foundation!

- All the foundations or governments of the earth are dislodged or fallen in decay *(Psalms 82:5).*
- His foundation is in His Holy Mountain *(Psalms 87:1).*

- If the foundations are destroyed, what can the righteous do *(Psalms 11:3)*?
- Jesus Christ is not only the foundation, but He is the chief cornerstone as well.

To whom coming, as unto a living stone, disallowed indeed of men, but chosen of God, and precious, Ye also, as lively stones, are built up a spiritual house, an holy priesthood, to offer up spiritual sacrifices, acceptable to God by Jesus Christ. Wherefore also it is contained in the scripture, Behold, I lay in Sion a chief corner stone, elect, precious: and he that believeth on him shall not be confounded. Unto you therefore which believe he is precious: but unto them which be disobedient, the stone which the builders disallowed, the same is made the head of the corner (1 Peter 2:4-6).

Further, the Apostle Paul says, *"And are built upon the foundation of the apostles and prophets, Jesus Christ himself being the chief corner stone" (Ephesians 2:20).* Jesus had a cadre of 12 men whom He trained and taught His doctrine in addition to the Old Testament prophets who spoke of the Messiah (the Christ). He sent these apostles into the world to preach Christ and Him crucified as the foundation of the church. *"For other foundation can no man lay than that is laid, which is Jesus Christ" (1 Corinthians 3:11).*

Who Builds This Church?

Notice, again, Jesus said that "Upon this rock, I will build MY Church, and the gates of hell shall not prevail against it" *(Matthew 16:18).* The church belongs to Christ. We have no claim of ownership at all. He paid for it with His blood. *"Take heed therefore unto yourselves, and to all the flock, over the which the Holy Ghost hath made you overseers, to feed the church of God, which HE HATH PURCHASED WITH HIS OWN BLOOD" (Acts 20:28)*. Christ has called some laborers to work with Him in this building, the CHURCH.

> *For we are labourers together with God: ye are God's husbandry, ye are God's building. According to the grace of God which is given unto me, as a wise masterbuilder, I have laid the foundation, and another buildeth thereon. But let every man take heed how he buildeth thereupon. For other foundation can no man lay than that is laid, which is Jesus Christ. Now if any man build upon this foundation gold, silver, precious stones, wood, hay, stubble; Every man's work shall be made manifest: for the day shall declare it, because it shall be revealed by fire; and the fire shall try every man's work of what sort it is. If any man's work abide which he hath built thereupon, he shall receive a reward. If any man's work shall be burned, he shall suffer loss: but he himself shall be saved; yet so as by fire (1 Corinthians 3:9-15).*

We then, as workers together with him, beseech you also that ye receive not the grace of God in vain" (2 Corinthians 6:1). We, the ministry, have been commissioned to labor in building a spiritual house and a holy habitation in which He has chosen to live. *"In whom all the building fitly framed together groweth unto an holy temple in the Lord: In whom ye also are builded together for an habitation of God through the Spirit (Ephesians 2:21-22).*

Zechariah speaks of Jesus as the BRANCH,

> *And speak unto him, saying, Thus speaketh the LORD of hosts, saying, Behold the man whose name is The BRANCH; and he shall grow up out of his place, and he shall build the temple of the LORD: Even he shall build the temple of the LORD; and he shall bear the glory, and shall sit and rule upon his throne; and he shall be a priest upon his throne: and the counsel of peace shall be between them both. And the crowns shall be to Helem, and to Tobijah, and to Jedaiah, and to Hen the son of Zephaniah, for a memorial in the temple of the LORD. And they that are far off shall come and build in the temple of the LORD, and ye shall know that the LORD of hosts hath sent me unto you. And this shall come to pass, if ye will diligently obey the voice of the LORD your God (Zechariah 6:12-15).*

Scripture reveals that Jesus Christ, the son of David, is not only THE BRANCH but the Messiah as well *(Isaiah 11:1; Jeremiah 23:5; Jeremiah 33:15-16; Zechariah 3:8)*. Notice, while the BRANCH is the builder, He has some help from those that are "far off" which would be the New Testament ministry beginning with the Apostles unto our present day ministers.

Christ Is The Head of The Body

The Principle of "headship" and rule was established in the Garden. Eve's desire was to be to her husband, "…and he shall rule over thee" *(Genesis 3:16)*. The husband is the head of the wife, so is Christ the head of the church *(Ephesians 5:23-24)*.

- *And hath put all things under his feet, and gave him to be the head over all things to the church, Which is his body, the fulness of him that filleth all in all (Ephesians 1:22-23).*

- *And he is the head of the body, the church: who is the beginning, the firstborn from the dead; that in all things he might have the preeminence (Colossians 1:18).*
- *And not holding the Head, from which all the body by joints and bands having nourishment ministered, and knit together, increaseth with the increase of God (Colossians 2:19).*

2

The Pastor

The role of the pastor is to maintain proper order and peace in the church. There must be ONE head and ONE source of authority. Since Christ is the head of the church, He has the right to choose and send, those who are to assist him in the governing and building process. As there is only one head of the church-Jesus Christ, likewise, there can be only one head of the local church-the pastor. The idea of co-pastors, where each has equal authority is confusion. The pastor may choose one or more assistants, but the pastor is the <u>one</u> who has the authority.

Who chooses the pastor of the local church? The Deacons, the Bishop, the church organization, or the church membership? Since the church belongs to God, then it stands to reason God will select the leader, overseer, or pastor. *"And I will give you pastors according to mine heart, which shall feed you with knowledge and understanding" (Jeremiah 3:15).* Here we see, it is God who will give pastors the responsibility to feed the people with knowledge and understanding. The person (male or female) to lead or be the under-shepherd of His church must be one the Chief Shepherd has chosen. **Every church should have something in the by-laws that governs the selection of the pastor**, keeping in mind that it is the church's desire to know God's mind and follow the will of His spirit. There are several avenues to follow and suggestions with try-outs to determine the will of God, which must be accompanied by prayer and fasting. The Bishop, Suffragan Bishop, District Elders and the Deacon Board of a local church may have suggestions for candidates to be considered. However, when a list of candidates has been agreed upon, they will be presented to the church membership for a vote. *"The lot is cast into the lap; but the whole disposing thereof is of the LORD"* (Proverb 16:33). In the final analysis, the membership votes their desire, but the Lord is the Spirit that makes the choice. To choose a pastor because of popularity, charisma, gender, or any reason other than God's will, is a disaster.

God's servants have four primary titles, each related yet functionally different from one another:

1. **PASTOR.** This is the feeder *(Jeremiah 3:15)*.
2. **SHEPHERD.** The caretaker and leader of the flock *(Ezekiel 34:2-10)*.
3. **WATCHMAN.** The guard and protector of the soul *(Hebrews 13:17)*.

4. **OVERSEER.** This is the one who rules or governs *(Matthew 24:45; Acts 20:28).*

The role of the pastor includes the following additional duties:

- Instructor, Teacher, Advisor
- Counselor
- Comforter, console those in sorrow
- Leader, Guide
- Example
- Judge, Disciplinarian, Corrector
- Protector
- Best friend, a helper in time of trouble
- Mediator

Role Of Pastor

Feeder. The following scriptural references outline the role of the pastor as:

- Peter is admonishing the pastors to "feed the flock of God" *(1 Peter 5:2-4).*
- God gives pastors to "feed with knowledge and understanding" *(Jeremiah 3:15).*
- The Priests lips are to keep knowledge and seek the law at God's mouth *(Malachi 2:7).*
- My people are destroyed for lack of knowledge [pastor failed to teach] (Hosea 4:6).
- Ezra prepared his heart to seek the law, both to do and to teach (Ezra 7:10).

THE PASTOR

- The teacher read distinctly and caused the people to understand *(Nehemiah 8:8)*.
- A servant (pastor) must be apt to teach *(2 Timothy 2:24)*.

Shepherd. The saints are God's flock and are referred to in both the Old and New Testaments as "SHEEP". The Shepherd is the caretaker of the sheep because they cannot care for themselves! They need someone called a *SHEPHERD* to watch over and take care of them. God, the CHIEF SHEPHERD, has provided for his flock an UNDER-SHEPHERD, who watches over and provides for the flock. As sheep, the saints are dependent on the under-shepherd for their survival. Please note the following scriptures:

- Jesus admonishes Peter to "feed my sheep". Be their shepherd (John 21:16).
- God would set shepherds over his flock *(Jeremiah 23:4)*.
- The saints are the sheep of His pasture *(Psalms 100:3)*.
- Take care of the Flock of God – the Holy Ghost made you overseers *(Acts 20:28)*.
- Feed the FLOCK of God and do not take advantage of them *(1 Peter 5:2-4)*.
- The shepherd is to attend the flock, if there is no shepherd the sheep will be scattered *(Ezekiel 34:2-12)*.
- The sheep are troubled because there is no shepherd (Zechariah 10:2).
- All of God' sheep are precious (Matthew 18:12-14).

Watchman. The watchman is the protector of God's people.

- God has made the pastor the watchman on the wall *(Ezekiel 3:17-21)*.
- Seek out the OLD paths, the people are to hearken to the watchman *(Jeremiah 6:16-17)*.
- Obey them that have rule over you – they watch for your soul *(Hebrews 13:17)*.

Overseer. Take heed to yourselves and the flock over which the Holy Ghost has made your *OVERSEERS (Acts 20:28)*. The overseer is one who is responsible for you to God.

Additional Roles

Instructor. There are times when the pastor is called upon to serve as an advisor or instructor. Being an instructor or advisor is one of the most thankless duties the pastor has to perform. To instruct those who are rebellious or self-willed can be, and often is, very frustrating. Human nature rebels against any advice that is contrary to its will. If one is unwilling to be instructed in small things, the devil will certainly take advantage of that soul and deceive the person to his or her destruction. If this is a problem with little issues, what will be the danger when more critical situations arise? The pastor must develop an attitude of *gentleness, meekness, and understanding* yet is firm in his/her instructions. Pastoral instruction is not designed to gain control over an individual or to show superiority but is given for the best interest of the individual's soul. Those who reject counsel will many times use the control issue as an excuse to refuse instruction.

THE PASTOR

1. In meekness instruct those who oppose themselves and help them to be saved *(2 Timothy 2:24-26)*.
2. Paul's counsel to Timothy was to reprove and rebuke with all long suffering *(2 Timothy 4:2-4)*.
3. Know them that labor among you and are over you in the Lord and (who) admonish you. Esteem them very highly in love for their work *(1 Thessalonians 5:12-13)*.
4. The people received the word as not from men, but the truth of God *(1 Thessalonians 2:13)*.
5. Paul said "I was gentle among you as a nurse cherishes her children" *(1 Thessalonians 2:7-8)*.

The pastor is to be an *EXAMPLE* of the believer *(1 Timothy 4:12)* and encourage the people to follow Christ as the pastor follows Christ *(1 Corinthians 11:1)*. Pastors are to seek to please God and to do His will and not be intimidated by the congregation by giving into their demands *(Galatians 1:10)*. The pastor must be a *PERCEPTIVE* person, possessing the spirit of discernment, so the watchman can detect the foul and unclean spirits that try to invade the congregation. Note, the following scriptures: *1 John 4:1; 1 Corinthians 12:10; Titus 1:9-11*.

God holds the pastor responsible for the well-being of the flock as he must give an account to God for each soul under his care. The people have the responsibility to listen and obey God's messenger if they are to be saved.

1. Obey the watchman for he *must give an account to God (Hebrews 13:17)*.

> **2.** The ministry is the angel of the Lord, Obey his voice *(Exodus 23:20-22).*

The responsible ministry or position in the church is referred to as the *"Angel of the Church" (Revelation 21-3:22).*

Helps. As the church grows, it becomes necessary for helpers to be provided for the pastor to carry out the work. The helpers are always under the authority of the pastor and are to carry out the assigned task outlined by the pastor. In the Old Testament, God realized Aaron could not carry out all the responsibilities of the Priesthood, so He gave the Levites to Aaron and his sons as a "gift" to help him in the work of the priesthood.

> *And I have given the Levites as a gift to Aaron and to his sons from among the children of Israel, to do the service of the children of Israel in the tabernacle of the congregation, and to make an atonement for the children of Israel: that there be no plague among the children of Israel, when the children of Israel come nigh unto the sanctuary (Numbers 8:19; Numbers 18:6).*

God's Ministerial Staff

God has provided a ministerial staff to establish His Church and to fulfill the work of the ministry in the church. They are Apostles, Prophets, Evangelists, Pastors, and Teachers.

> **1.** *And he gave some, apostles; and some, prophets; and some, evangelists and some, pastors and teachers; For the perfecting of the saints, for the work of the ministry, for the edifying of the body of Christ: Till we all come in the unity of the faith, and of the knowledge of the Son of God, unto a*

> *perfect man, unto the measure of the stature of the fulness of Christ (Ephesians 4:11-13).*
>
> **2.** *And God hath set some in the church, first apostles, secondarily prophets, thirdly teachers, after that miracles, then gifts of healings, helps, government, diversities of tongues (1 Corinthians 12:28).*

Apostles. The first Apostles consisted of 12 men chosen by Jesus and were the earliest staff members of the New Testament Church. Jesus personally trained these first Apostles in the Teachings which is referred to as the "Apostles Doctrine". Our "Faith" is known as the "Apostles Doctrine" does not mean the Apostles originated it, but that they were commissioned by Jesus Christ to establish it throughout the world for all people. Jesus alone is the Author and Finisher of our faith *(Hebrews 12:2)*. The Apostles only carried out what they had received from Him and were to pass on to us *(2 Timothy 2:2)*. Also, they were men who had an intimate contact with the ministry of Jesus and were first-hand witnesses of all that Jesus said and did during the three years or so of His ministry. One qualification of an apostle was that the individual had to have seen and been with Jesus. Paul, a late appointee, testifies that he was "as one born out of due time" but he too had seen Christ in the deserts of Arabia and was instructed by Him. This office does not exist in today's ministry even though some may call themselves apostles, which only expresses a position of oversight *(1 Corinthians 15:8)*. The Pentecostal Assemblies of the World forbids any of its ministers (i.e., Bishop, Suffragan Bishop, District Elder, or Elder) to assume the title apostle. The Apostles wrote the record of the life of Jesus and His teachings. They established the doctrine of the Church for their day and ours. The Apostles' writings were the results of the inspired anointing of the Holy Ghost that formed the New Testament Scriptures. No one since them has the authority to preach or establish any doctrine or teaching other than that which is already established by the Apostles' record. Paul states, *"But though we, or an angel from heaven, preach any other gospel unto you than that which we have preached unto you let him be accursed" (Galatians 1:8)*. There are no modern day scripture writers.

Prophets. The office of prophet is not to be thought of as someone foretelling the future in some manner. The Old Testament prophets spoke as God anointed them to speak of things to come concerning the coming Messiah and the coming Kingdom as well as the judgment of the current conditions of their day. We have no Isaiahs, Jeremiahs, or Daniels serving today. Who, then, are the prophets of the New Testament ministry? This office refers to the preaching ministry, those who carry the good news of the Gospel. In other words, the New Testament prophets are those who are not pastors, but called by God to preach His word, the word already recorded for our use. Many consider themselves prophets in that they speak of things to come, "whom to marry" or some special calling for an individual, which is rarely true and only causes confusion. They say, "God told me thus-and-so" when in reality it is the spirit of deceit in their own heart. Here are additional scriptures: *Jeremiah 14:14; 23:21-26; Deuteronomy 13:1-4; Ezekiel 13:3.*

Evangelist. The office of the evangelist is one who takes the Gospel message to people who have not heard of the Lord Jesus Christ. The role is critical because without them many would never hear the message of salvation. Phillip is THE example of an evangelist in the Book of Acts as he is referred to as "The evangelist" (*Acts 21:8*). Most of the preachers who come to our churches to hold revivals and who we call evangelists, are not in fact true evangelists but preachers who are holding meetings for us. If there are unsaved people in the congregation, it is the evangelist's responsibility to preach the gospel and not to set the church straight. This is the responsibility of the pastor. A true evangelist will go where no one else has gone to seek converts for the Kingdom of God. When they are able to help someone be saved, then the pastor is the one to feed and instruct the soul.

Pastors and teachers. The office of the pastor was previously defined as the feeder, under-shepherd, watchman, and overseer. This is a combined function of the pastor's role. The pastor must be "apt to teach" and to do the work of an evangelist (1 Timothy 3:2; 2 Timothy 4:5). The teacher is not a separate ministry in the church but is part of the pastor's duty. All teaching responsibility belongs to the pastoral role. The pastor may have a staff to assist, such as Sunday school teachers, teachers for the women and young people, or other specially assigned teaching functions, but in reality the pastor is accountable for what is taught in the local church. Those who are called into the pastor's service to minister in the local pastor's church cannot rely on their talents, but must be under the direction of the Holy Ghost and deliver the message God has desired to communicate with His people. In other words, the minister does not choose the message, but must wait until it is given by God because the minister is God's communication link with His people.

- *Not that we are sufficient of ourselves to think anything as of ourselves; but our sufficiency is of God; Who also hath made us able ministers of the New Testament; not of the letter, but of the spirit: for the letter killeth, but the spirit giveth life (2 Corinthians 3:5-6).*
- *If any man speak, let him speak as the oracles of God; if any man minister, let him do it as of the ability which God giveth: that God in all things may be glorified through Jesus Christ, to whom be praise and dominion for ever and ever. Amen (1 Peter: 4:11).*
- *For the priest's lips should keep knowledge, and they should seek the law at his mouth: for he is the messenger of the LORD of hosts (Malachi 2:7).*

3
Church Membership

"Jesus answered, Verily, verily, I say unto thee, Except a man be born of water and of the Spirit, he cannot enter into the kingdom of God' (John 3:5).

How does one become a member of God's church? One does not merely become a member of the flock of God simply by church attendance. One must be born into the church *(John 3:3-5)*. Jesus gave clear instructions on how one becomes a member of the Body of Christ. The teaching of the Apostle Paul is very clear about not only the necessity of being born again but states without the Holy Ghost one cannot be part of God's body or family. The only tool the ministry has is the Gospel of Jesus Christ. Preaching the Gospel becomes the divine dragnet for reaching out to anyone who will respond and believe the Gospel.

Note the following scriptures verify the need of the New Birth experience, water baptism and being filled with the Holy Ghost, without which one cannot claim a relationship with God:

- *"Jesus answered and said unto him, Verily, verily, I say unto thee, except a man be born again, he cannot see the kingdom of God. Nicodemus saith unto him, How can a man be born when he is old? can he enter the second time into his mother's womb, and be born? Jesus answered, Verily, verily, I say unto thee, Except a man be born of water and of the Spirit, he cannot enter into the kingdom of God" (John 3:3-5).*

- *"But ye are not in the flesh, but in the Spirit, if so be that the Spirit of God dwell in you. Now if any man have not the Spirit of Christ, he is none of his" (Romans 8:9).*

- *"Nevertheless the foundation of God standeth sure, having this seal, The Lord knoweth them that are his. And, Let everyone that nameth the name of Christ depart from iniquity" (2 Timothy 2:19).*

- *"And of Zion it shall be said, This and that man was born in her: and the highest himself shall establish her. The LORD shall count, when he writeth up the people, that this man was born there. Selah" (Psalms. 87:5-6).*

There are those who refuse to comply with God's program but work and labor under the belief they are in God's Kingdom. Their labor is in vain because God never knew them as part of His family (the New Birth) and in the end they will be cast into the abyss of destruction.

Not everyone that saith unto me, Lord, Lord, shall enter into the kingdom of heaven; but he that doeth the will of my Father which is in heaven. Many will say to me in that day, Lord, Lord, have we not prophesied in thy name? and in thy name have cast out devils? And in thy name done many wonderful works? And then will I profess unto them, I never knew you: depart from me, ye that work iniquity (Matthew 7:21-23).

God's Gospel call is to "who-so-ever-will, let him come." Of those called, not everyone will respond with a believing heart. Isn't it strange that from some large families only one or two choose to be saved? Then again there are very large families where all the family members are in the church. It depends on each INDIVIDUAL RESPONSE. Every soul is separate and distinct and must answer to God for themselves. All souls must individually make a decision to be saved and to walk with God. So how does God build His church? One soul at a time. *"And the Lord added to the church daily such as should be saved" (Acts 2:47).*

"God setteth the solitary in families: he bringeth out those which are bound with chains: but the rebellious dwell in a dry land" (Psalms 68:6). Notice, those who rebel or refuse to believe the Gospel or hear the Shepherd, dwell in a dry land. There is no instruction, no joy, no peace, no hope, no life in the dry land. As a result their soul dries up and is destroyed. Further, the scriptures state, *"Yet setteth he the poor on high from affliction, and maketh him families like a flock" (Psalms 107:41).* Notice, God calls out single individuals, the solitary, who were

bound with chains. A single sheep left by itself would soon be devoured by the predator or wolf, so for safety the sheep are placed with other single sheep to make a family. He sets or places them in families, the local church, and then groups these families together as a flock. Think of many individual sheep being called and placed together in a family (the local church).

Once the family has been established, God gathers other solitary sheep and brings them to the local church. Over this family the Chief Shepherd provides an under-shepherd or pastor to feed, teach, and protect them from the wolves who would steal and kill the sheep. All local churches being a family are gathered together to make the FLOCK of God. In others words, all the local assemblies throughout the world (God's church is a world wide church comprised of all nations, tongues and peoples make up THE BODY OF CHRIST and are called the FLOCK of God. *"And I will give you pastors according to mine heart, which shall feed you with knowledge and understanding" (Jeremiah 3:15).*

Governing Authority in the Church

Pastors govern the local churches. *"Who then is a faithful and wise servant, whom his lord <u>hath made</u> ruler over his household, to give them meat in due season? Blessed is that servant, whom his lord when he cometh shall find so doing" (Matthew 24:45-46).* As noted in the preceding Scripture, God has made the faithful and wise SERVANT (the pastor) to be ruler or governor of His household. For the church to grow, prosper, be blessed, and fruitful, the pastor must be <u>chosen by God</u> and not chosen through OUR political systems. The Pastor is the head and one leading voice of the local church. Moreover, the pastor is God's appointed overseer and serves as the watchman, ruler, feeder, and is the under shepherd. Whereas the deacons and the other branches of the ministry serve as helpers (ordained or not) and do not have the pastoral authority. The auxiliary departments are not independent entities of the church but are under the direct supervision of the pastor.

The **PASTOR ALONE** bears the responsibility of governing and accountability of the church and its membership. The deacons in the church are not "money counters," but are the pastor's helpers in carrying out the policy of the church as outlined by the pastor. They assist him in the administration of the church. The pastor is the leader and has the vision, and all authority emanates from the position. The pastor must be a strong leader to maintain the true Apostolic Doctrine and standards of holiness in the church. The pastor must be able to resist the efforts by some factions to control or usurp the pastoral authority.

God does not deal with any other position in the church in the same manner as He deals with the pastor. We do not want to imply that the pastor is of the same rank as Moses, but we see that God deals with the local church leader differently than anyone else. Please review the scriptures where Miriam and Aaron challenged Moses by saying, *"Hath the Lord indeed spoken ONLY by Moses? hath he not spoken also by us* (v. 2)?" Then, God replies in verses 6-8,

And he said, Hear now my words: If there be a prophet among you, I the LORD will make myself known unto him in a vision, and will speak unto him in a dream. My servant Moses is not so, who is faithful in all mine house. With him will I speak mouth to mouth, even apparently, and not in dark speeches; and the similitude of the LORD shall he behold: wherefore then were ye not afraid to speak against my servant Moses (Numbers 12:1-8)?

God does not speak to pastors face to face these days, but He speaks to them by His Spirit in a manner different from all other members of the church. Others may communicate with God and feel the presence of His Spirit; but to the pastor, God reveals His will and purpose.

If one fails to be subject to the pastor that God has provided, then one puts his or her soul in grave danger. Further, anyone who is not subject to the pastor cannot hold any position in the church, nor can they be a leader of God's heritage. When one refuses to listen to the pastor of a local church it is as the individual elevates oneself ABOVE church authority. This is SIN! Rebellion against church authority has happened in the Old Testament and still exists today. When Korah rebelled against Moses with those who were influenced by his behavior, there was a devastating end result *(Numbers 16:3-10; 2 Peter 2:10)*. In dealing with the situation of rebellion, the pastor must do all in his or her power to help those who oppose the pastoral leadership and church authority with all long-suffering and meekness. Scripture says,

And the servant of the Lord must not strive; but be gentle unto all men, apt to teach, patient, in meekness instructing those that oppose themselves; if God peradventure will give them repentance to the acknowledging of the truth; and that they may recover themselves out of the snare of the devil, who are taken captive by him at his will (2 Timothy 2:24-26).

The Holy Ghost makes the pastor the overseer and one of the

primary pastoral duties is to feed the flock of God. The pastor then is the ruler or governor of those individuals God has sent into the local church. They are under his/her authority and must be subject to him. However the pastor is not a dictator or one to abuse the sheep, but he is to be gentle, loving, and kind, while at the same time be firm.

The elders which are among you I exhort, who am also an elder, and a witness of the sufferings of Christ, and also a partaker of the glory that shall be revealed: Feed the flock of God which is among you, taking the oversight thereof, <u>not by constraint, but</u> willingly; not for filthy lucre, but of a ready mind; <u>Neither as being lords over God's heritage</u>, but being ensamples to the flock (1 Peter 5:1-3).

Note the following scriptural references:

- Take heed to the flock which the Holy Ghost has made you overseers *(Acts 20:28)*.
- Feed the flock of God – taking the oversight but not as Lords over God's heritage *(1 Peter 5:1-3)*.
- Jesus is the Chief Shepherd and the pastor is the appointed under shepherd *(1 Peter 5:4)*.
- Words of the wise by "masters of assemblies" *(Ecclesiastes 12:11)*.
- The pastor LEADS, the flock is to follow as the leader follows Christ *(1 Corinthians 11:1)*.

Qualifications of Pastors

This is a true saying, If a man desire the office of a bishop, he desireth a good work. A bishop then must be blameless, the husband of one wife, vigilant, sober, of good behaviour, given to hospitality, apt to teach; Not given to wine, no striker, not greedy of filthy lucre; but patient, not a brawler, not covetous; One that ruleth well his own house, having his children in subjection with all gravity; (For if a man know not how to rule his own house, how shall he take care of the church of God?) Not a novice, lest being lifted up with pride he fall into the condemnation of the devil. Moreover he must have a good report of them which are without; lest he fall into reproach and the snare of the devil (1 Timothy 3:1-7; Titus 1:5-11).

The term "BISHOP" is used in these verses is synonymous to the term OVERSEER and refers to a pastor. Today's usage of the term BISHOP is used in the ecclesiastical sense as the overseer of a Diocese or a group of local churches. The person who aspires to the office of Pastor must be one who is above reproach, experienced and has knowledge of the doctrine, have a good report from within and outside the church, have his/her family under control and is able to minister effectively.

The Pastor with the ministry is essential to each member in the Body of Christ. Remember, the pastor with the local ministry is God's communicator to His flock. In one sense of the word, the pastor is the life link between the individual's soul and God. If God sends His Word through the anointed ministry and the sheep fail to hear or rebel against the message then, their soul is in danger. Spiritual life is dependent on the ministry in the church. Without the ministry, one would not be able to hear the gospel preached. They would have no way of communication with God or to be instructed by Him. Angels are not preaching the gospel. As exemplified in the subsequent scriptures, Cornelius is a man who moved heaven to dispatch an angelic messenger to him with instructions to send for Peter, the minister who had the message of salvation *(Acts 10:1-48)*.

The Apostle Paul speaks of the necessity of the ministry,

Who then is Paul, and who is Apollos, <u>but ministers by whom ye believed</u>, even as the Lord gave to every man?" (1 Corinthians 3:5) And again, *"For whosoever shall call upon the name of the Lord shall be saved. How then shall they call on him in whom they have not believed? and how shall they believe in him of whom they have not heard? and how shall they hear without a preacher? (Romans 10:13-14)*

- The minister is an ambassador for Christ. They have the "WORD" of reconciliation *(2 Corinthians 5:18-20)*.
- You received ministers not as men, but as in truth and messengers of the word of God *(1 Thessalonians 2:13)*.

Every saved person must be a member of a local assembly! No individual can pastor himself or herself but must have someone over them to watch for their souls. Every child of God has to have someone over them. As a church member, the pastor is the overseer and watchman. The pastor is not a police officer that monitors your every move but is the watchman of your soul and the instructor of your salvation. According to the practice of the Pentecostal Assemblies of the World, the Pastor has the District Elder along with the Suffragan Bishop as overseer. These officers have the Diocesan Bishop as watchman and authority and the Diocesan Bishop, in turn, has the Board of Bishops as overseer. Everyone in God's kingdom must be accountable to someone. Note the following scriptural references:

- The pastor must give an account of every soul under his/her responsibility *(Hebrews 13:7, 17)*.
- Caution, DO NOT rebel against the established authority in the church *(Isaiah 1:19-20)*.
- Eventually, each member of God's church must give an account *(Romans 14:12)*.

4
Church Rule

For the church to function properly, the pastor must have some assistants in the governance of the church. Each local assembly is a sovereign unit with a single head and its own form of government, provided it does not conflict with the scriptures and follows the guidelines of the Bible. *"Now ye are the body of Christ and members in particular. And God hath set some in the church, first apostles, secondarily prophets, thirdly teachers, after that miracles, then gifts of healings, helps, governments, diversities of tongues" (1 Corinthians (12:27-28).*

- Know them that are over you in the Lord and esteem them highly *(1 Thessalonians 5:12-13)*.

- God promised to send an angel before you – obey his voice (Exodus 23:20-22).

"Let the elders that rule well be counted worthy of double honour, especially they who labour in the word and doctrine" *(1 Timothy 5:17)*. There are two kinds of elders in the church:

1. Those who deal with the Word and Doctrine (the ministry).
2. Those who rule by other means, assisting the pastor (deacons).

The term *elder* has two meanings: first, an aged person who is respected for their wisdom; second, one who is in a ruling or governing position. Frequently in the Pentecostal Assemblies of the World, the term elder is applied to the ministry; however, in other organizations, elder could mean anyone in authority in the church.

The ministry and deacons are the only officers created by the New Testament. Helpers in the church, including the auxiliary departments, church secretary or administrator, treasurer, trustees, and any other officers not ordained by God but those roles are essential to the operation of the church as long as scripture is not violated. These additional roles have become necessary because of the growth of the modern day church and the development of various departments designed to broaden the needs of today's congregations. Legal requirements and property ownership has made the office of trustee necessary. Record keeping for corporate reporting have made the roles of secretary and treasurer necessary. Rules and regulations imposed by government agencies have affected many of the operations in church administration. Keep in mind that these new offices are not spiritual offices, but are not necessary for the function of the Kingdom of God. While there are no scriptural references, God permits them in the government of the church. Nonetheless, the Old Testament scribes kept records of events and the period, and recorded the name of members of Israel by tribes. See *Ezra 2:62* and *1 Chronicles chapters 1 through 9*. The spiritual offices are limited to the Ministry and all of its branches, and are responsible for the preaching, teaching, doctrine, and administration of the church and the deacons who assists the pastor in the administrative duties.

5
Role of Deacons

The office of deacon came into existence when local church assemblies were formed and the role was established to support the pastor in ruling the local church. Deacons receive their authority and power FROM the pastor and are to function as the pastor directs them. The positions, along with other helpers in the church, assist the pastor in implementing church policies initiated by the pastor. In other words, every office in the church derives its power, authority, and duties from the pastor. The pastor alone is responsible and no one else. All departments of the church are subject to the pastor. The pastor is not a coordinator, seeking direction from a committee or the congregation, but all church policies begin with the pastor and filters down through the other departments for implementation. Helpers in the church must be those who are FAITHFUL, TRUSTWORTHY (dependable), and in full HARMONY with the pastor, doctrine, and the church policy.

The title "Deacon" comes from the Greek word "diakonus" which means "servant" or one who serves. The requirements of the deacon are very similar to those of the pastor. They are more than "money counters," as is the common belief practiced in many churches. The office of deacon is imperative in assisting the pastor. The deacon, while not a minister, must know the doctrine and be able to exhort and defend the teachings of the Apostles. The deacons or deaconesses are to be special men and women who are willing to be subordinate to the pastor and defend the pastor when people attack for no justifiable reason. The deacon, along with the pastor, is the watchman of the souls of God's people. The term first was mentioned in *Philippians 1:1* and later in *1 Timothy 3:8-13*:

Likewise must the deacons be grave, not doubletongued, not given to much wine, not greedy of filthy lucre; Holding the mystery of the faith in a pure conscience. And let these also first be proved; then let them use the office of a deacon, being found blameless. Even so must their wives be grave, not slanderers, sober, faithful in all things. Let the deacons be the husbands of one wife, ruling their children and their own houses well. For they that have used the office of a deacon well purchase to themselves a good degree, and great boldness in the faith which is in Christ Jesus (1 Timothy 3:8-13).

The spouses of pastors, ministers, and deacons play an important part in the church structure, not because of any authority bestowed upon the wives, but the examples they set before the congregation. The qualifications of the deacon is one who is first proved and is found to be well established in the faith, sober, not one to spread gossip or false accusations. The deacon is in control of his home by ruling it well. His marriage is stable, being the husband of one wife and his children are subject to his authority.

God is a sovereign being and recognizes the awesome responsibilities of His church. He knows that one person is not able to provide all that is necessary for taking care of His people. Moses received some good advice from his father-in-law, Jethro, which encouraged him to deputize helpers (*Exodus 18*). After this, God authorized Moses to select some helpers to assist him. No pastor is capable of taking care of God's people alone. In spite of the personal ego and self-imagined ability, a pastor needs someone to assist with God's program. A pastor cannot teach every Sunday school class or reach every single person all the time. Pastors need helpers. Depending on the size of the church, the number of helpers will vary. As in the case of Moses, God took some of the spirit of Moses and put it on the seventy assistants who were chosen to help judge the congregation. Those helpers in the church must also have the mind of the pastor and, in a similar manner, have the pastor's spirit on them.

And the LORD said unto Moses, Gather unto me seventy men of the elders of Israel, whom thou knowest to be the elders of the people, and officers over them; and bring them unto the tabernacle of the congregation, that they may stand there with thee. And I will come down and talk with thee there: and I will take of the spirit which is upon thee, and will put it upon them; and they shall bear the burden of the people with thee, that thou bear it not thyself alone. And the LORD came down in a cloud, and spake unto him, and took of the spirit that was upon him, and gave it unto the seventy elders: and it came to pass, that, when the spirit rested upon them, they prophesied, and did not cease (Numbers 11:16-17, 25).

God authorized the seventy elders to assist in the judgment of the congregation and he gave Aaron, the high priest, a GIFT in the form of the Levites, who would help in the temple duties.

And I have given the Levites as a GIFT to Aaron and to his sons from among the children of Israel, to do the service of the children of Israel in the tabernacle of the congregation, and to make an atonement for the children of Israel: that there be no plague among the children of Israel, when the children of Israel come nigh unto the sanctuary (Numbers 8:19; 18:6).

Furthermore, Paul spoke of those women who labored with him in the gospel *(Philippians 4:3)*. Most pastors must depend on faithful women in the church. Women are able to perform many helpful duties for the church and are often the first to get things moving toward the pastor's vision.

6
Judgment In The Church

"For the time has come that judgment must begin at the house of God, and if it first begin at us, what shall the end be of them that obey not the gospel of God?" (1 Peter 4:17).

The authority to judge members of the church is well established in the Old and New Testaments. God's church must be kept clean of sin, defilement, and corruption. However, the objective is not to punitively punish the wrongdoer, but to reveal wrong and to save the soul rather than destroy it. To excommunicate members is the course of last resort and only when they fail to repent properly or refuse to submit to the authority of the church; only then are they to be dismissed from the congregation. *"He, that being often reproved hardeneth his neck, shall suddenly be destroyed, and that without remedy" (Proverbs 29:1).* Personal feelings MUST NOT enter into the judgment process.

Where there are people, there will be problems to be resolved. Where there are laws, there will be those who for one reason or another violate those laws. The arbitrating process is an effort to make a distinction between right and wrong, and to help those who have violated the scripture be reconciled to God. Disputes and offenses often arise in the church, and there must be some procedure whereby these disputes can be resolved. Sometimes discipline is necessary to enforce the law and to make the transgressor aware of the demands of God. Sin is an ugly specter that severely affects the church and if allowed to go unpunished will eventually destroy the integrity of the church. Those who sin must be judged and rehabilitated, if possible. It must be the objective of the judges to bring about repentance and redemption of the transgressor at all times. God is not a punitive God and takes no pleasure in the death of the wicked, but is always striving to bring one to repentance. Without repentance, there can be no forgiveness.

Have I any pleasure at all that the wicked should die? Saith the Lord GOD: and not that he should return from his ways, and live? For I have no pleasure in the death of him that dieth, saith the Lord GOD: wherefore turn yourselves, and live ye (Ezekiel 18:23, 32).

Further, "*The Lord is not slack concerning his promise, as some men count slackness; but is longsuffering to us-ward, not willing that any should perish, but that all should come to repentance"* (2 Peter 3:9). There are guidelines for the church judgment procedure. Jesus, when He dealt with the woman taken in adultery, did not justify the woman but simply gave her a reprieve because the judges were not qualified to judge her.

> *So when they continued asking him, he lifted up himself, and said unto them, 'He that is without sin among you, let him first cast a stone at her.' And again he stooped down, and wrote on the ground. And they which heard it, being convicted by their own conscience, went out one by one, beginning at the eldest, even unto the last: and Jesus was left alone, and the woman standing in the midst (John 8:7-9).*

It is evident those who judge must be free of sin and guiltless. Review the scriptural references below:

- *Deuteronomy 16:18-19*
- *Exodus 18:21*

The church courtroom consists of the pastor, the chief judge, along with the deacons or deaconesses and any other elders appointed by the pastor. Let us examine God's requirements for judging. There are ministries that teach church leadership has no rights to judge; yet, the authority is invested in the church to deal with those matters that offend God or one another. It is God's mercy that provides the platform for a trial for the guilty in order to redeem them, if possible. God puts Himself in the midst of judges as illustrated in the following scriptural reference:

> *And I charged your judges at that time, saying, Hear the causes between your brethren, and judge righteously between every man and his brother, and the stranger that is with him. Ye shall not*

respect persons in judgment; but ye shall hear the small as well as the great; ye shall not be afraid of the face of man; for the judgment is God's: and the cause that is too hard for you, bring it unto me, and I will hear it (*Deuteronomy 1:16-17*).

Moses instructed the judges regarding their conduct. They were to hear each case fairly, to be absolutely impartial, and not be intimidated by the fierceness of man's countenance. The judgment or decision rendered, if according to the law, was the judgment of God and He stands by the judges to enforce the verdict.

It was the duty of Ezra to set judges and magistrates among the people. These judges needed to know the law and those who were not knowledgeable were to be taught.

And thou, Ezra, after the wisdom of thy God, that is in thine hand, set magistrates and judges, which may judge all the people that are beyond the river, all such as know the laws of thy God; and teach ye them that know them not. And whosoever will not do the law of thy God, and the law of the king, let judgment be executed speedily upon him, whether it be unto death, or to banishment, or to confiscation of goods, or to imprisonment (Ezra 7:25-26).

There were various punishments for different crimes. God has commissioned judges to <u>judge for him</u>. The judges are to carry out the adjudicating procedure as though God Himself is there.

And he set judges in the land throughout all the fenced cities of Judah, city by city, And said to the judges, Take heed what ye do: <u>for ye judge not for man, but for the LORD</u>, who is with you in the judgment. Wherefore now let the fear of the LORD be upon you;

take heed and do it: for there is no iniquity with the LORD our God, nor respect of persons, nor taking of gifts (2 Chronicle 19:5-7).

The judges are not to be a respecter of persons; that is, to permit personalities, status, or race to interfere with the ruling process nor to be enticed by gifts or payoff. It is a serious thing to be in a position to judge another individual. Therefore, God has given help to those who are called to be judges.

In that day shall the LORD of hosts be for a crown of glory, and for a diadem of beauty, unto the residue of his people, <u>And for a spirit of judgment to him that sitteth in judgment</u>, and for strength to them that turn the battle to the gate (Isaiah 28:5-6).

No one is exempt from the judicial process of the church. We either will judge ourselves or repent of our mistakes or the church will hold us accountable. The church is not one person but consists of a judicial court of the pastor, deacons, and the portion of the ministerial staff that the pastor appoints. The church has authority over its members from the time of the member's New Birth experience unto death or the rapture. The backslider or excommunicated cannot escape the judicial process of the church. Remember, the church operates under the authority of God and holds each member accountable to the pastor. Generally when one sins or backslides, the local assembly that the person previously attended is the same place he or she returns to if the person is to be restored in fellowship with God. In short, the door one leaves from is the same door he or she must re-enter if fellowship with God—and the congregation--is to be restored. *"But why dost thou judge thy brother? or why dost thou set at nought thy brother? for we shall all stand before the judgment seat of Christ" (Romans 14:10).*

The subsequent scriptures demonstrate our future responsibility as children of God and the danger of using a judicial procedure other than the church.

> *Dare any of you, having a matter against another, go to law before the unjust, and not before the saints? <u>Do ye not know that the saints shall judge the world? and if the world shall be judged by you, are ye unworthy to judge the smallest matters? Know ye not that we shall judge angels? how much more things that pertain to this life?</u> If then ye have judgments of things pertaining to this life, set them to judge who are least esteemed in the church. I speak to your shame. Is it so, that there is not a wise man among you? no, not one that shall be able to judge between his brethren? But brother goeth to law with brother, and that before the unbelievers. Now therefore there is utterly a fault among you, because ye go to law one with another. Why do ye not rather take wrong? why do ye not rather suffer yourselves to be defrauded? (1 Corinthians 6:1-7)*

There are two principles expressed in the above verses. The first principle, problems that exist between members of the Body of Christ are to be adjudicated within the church forum that is the judicial court of the church. The procedure is outlined in the New Testament (Matthew 18:15-20). There is a <u>strong warning</u> for "brethren" not to go to the civil law for redress of their grievances, but to the church. Paul chastised them in irony by saying "Do you not have qualified persons in your midst? Do you take the least, the most unqualified, to set up as your judges?" The implied answer is a resounding NO! To reinforce his statement he adds, "I speak to your shame." Surely there is a wise brother among you that is capable of judging between brethren. It is better to take wrong for the glory of God than to take your brother to law before the unjust judge. Until officials of the church are ready to enforce this principle, God's Church will suffer a tremendous loss of credibility and members who need help will be unwilling to come to the church for help.

The second principle, the future responsibility of the saints will be to judge the world. What an awesome responsibility that will be! If the judging process is not perfected now in this life, how will the church be trusted to take on this tremendous responsibility in the future? Often, it has been said that the church is doing *on the job training;* that is, qualifying itself for the time yet to be revealed. Paul adds, do you not know we shall judge angels? How much more the things we face now.

Similarly, there should also be weight given to one's conduct in ensuring that the qualities of being a judge are being properly honed. This brings up the following: Who do we fellowship with in the church and how should we treat them? Consider what Paul has further said:

I wrote unto you in an epistle not to company with fornicators: Yet not altogether with the fornicators of this world, or with the covetous, or extortioners, or with idolaters; for then must ye needs go out of the world. But now I have written unto you not to keep company, if any man that is called a brother be a fornicator, or covetous, or an idolater, or a railer, or a drunkard, or an extortioner; with such an one no not to eat. For what have I to do to judge them also that are without? do not ye judge them that are *within? But them that are without God judgeth. <u>Therefore put away from among yourselves that wicked person</u> (1 Corinthians 5:9-13).*

Sin, when discovered, must be judged and some action taken. The above scriptures clearly states that we are not to fellowship with those among us who are guilty of the sins outlined above. Remember, the church's job is not to primarily excommunicate, but to redeem, if possible. However, if the one who is in sin refuses to abide by the standard of the church, then the person is to be put out of fellowship and God will deal with the person.

The church's judgment authority does not cover the evildoers in this world, but it covers those guilty of sin in the church. The verdict, therefore, is to put away from you that wicked person. Again, if sin is allowed to go without being judged, the whole church will in time be corrupted. See Paul's judgment of the man in the Corinthian church.

It is reported commonly that there is fornication among you, and such fornication as is not so much as named among the Gentiles, that one should have his father's wife. And ye are puffed up, and have not rather mourned, that he that hath done this deed might be taken away from among you. For I verily, as absent in body, but present in spirit, have judged already, as though I were present, concerning him that hath so done this deed, In the name of our Lord Jesus Christ, when ye are gathered together, and my spirit, with the power of our Lord Jesus Christ, To deliver such an one unto Satan for the destruction of the flesh, that the spirit may be saved in the day of the Lord Jesus. Your glorying is not good. Know ye not that a little leaven leaveneth the whole lump? (1 Corinthians 5:1-6)

> *Moreover if thy brother shall trespass against thee, go and tell him his fault between thee and him alone: if he shall hear thee, thou hast gained thy brother. But if he will not hear thee, then take with thee one or two more, that in the mouth of two or three witnesses every word may be established. And if he shall neglect to hear them, tell it unto the church: but if he neglect to hear the church, let him be unto thee as an heathen man and a publican. Verily I say unto you, Whatsoever ye shall bind on earth shall be bound in heaven: and whatsoever ye shall loose on earth shall be loosed in heaven. Again I say unto you, That if two of you shall agree on earth as touching any thing that they shall ask, it shall be done for them of my Father which is in heaven. For where two or three are gathered together in my name, there am I in the midst of them (Matthew 18:15-20).*

Note, the verses describe the procedure to resolve disputes between members of the church and the forum in which issues are judged. It is not a small church gathering for service, but the judicial court in which the Lord Himself will attend in Spirit. Also it indicates the smallest number to conduct the judicial process, two – the pastor and one other. These scriptures describe a dispute between two individuals, brothers or sisters in the church. One is the transgressor, and the other is the offended party. Let the two judges get together with the offended party in order to meet the transgressor and counsel him about the transgression. The objective is for the transgressor to acknowledge his wrong and repent so the offended person can extend forgiveness. If this does not work, get a witness who knows the matter and that individual try to persuade the offender to admit wrong and repent. As a final attempt to resolve the issue, let them bring the dispute to the church (the pastor and deacons). Let them work to get the admission of wrong; however, if the transgressor refuses to abide by the church's ruling, then the individual should be put out as unworthy of fellowship.

Now, the effect of this action places the offender in jeopardy of losing his soul. He is bound by the judgment of the church. He that is bound or judged (by the church) is bound or judged in heaven. He that is set free of the earth (by the church) is set free in heaven. God recognized the church's authority to judge and responds accordingly to their judgment. Further, in the judging process, <u>Christ Jesus is the invisible person on the judicial board</u> and His Spirit influences the judges. It is not a personal thing but the Spirit of Christ. Since this is the magnitude of the matter great the judges must exercise discretion and spiritual insight because an individual's soul is at stake. The authority and the power of the church illustrated and supported by the following scripture: *"Whosoever sins ye remit, they are remitted unto them; and whosesoever sins ye retain, they are retained"* (John 20:23). Remember Jesus said that this authority is in the church, not given to persons, but those ordained by God to judge. Similarly, in our judicial system, the common person is not free to judge or to execute a given sentence; nevertheless, this authority is left to the proper judge to exercise. Likewise in the church, we are not to judge one another in the pews; rather, such authority is left to the church judicial court to exercise.

Consider the additional scriptural references:
- Those who have rejected God's Word have in fact rejected

God *(1 Samuel 15:22-26)*.
- God will judge those who despise government *(2 Peter 2:9-10)*.
- The soul who sins through ignorance and the presumptuous sin *(Numbers 15:27-31)*.
- Those who acted presumptuously were judged by God *(Deuteronomy 1:43-45)*.

Judgment Procedure

There are rules to govern the church court judges, and there are rules to govern the adjudicating procedures as well. One cannot be brought to the judgment forum without some accusation. Because one is accused does not mean one is guilty. Proof or witnesses must establish the person's guilt. It is the judge's responsibility to determine the validity of the witnesses, and the evidence presented. The following scriptures will outline the procedures God instituted for the judges of Israel. These same procedures are in force today if the judgment is to be a righteous judgment.

If there be found among you, within any of thy gates which the LORD thy God giveth thee, man or woman, that hath wrought wickedness in the sight of the LORD thy God, in transgressing his covenant, And hath gone and served other gods, and worshipped them, either the sun, or moon, or any of the host of heaven, which I have not commanded; And it be told thee, and thou hast heard of it, and enquired diligently, and, behold, it be true, and the thing certain, that such abomination is wrought in Israel: Then shalt thou *bring forth that man or that woman, which have committed that wicked thing, unto thy gates, even that man or that woman, and shalt stone them with stones, till they die. <u>At the mouth of two witnesses, or three witnesses</u>, shall he that is worthy of death be put to death; <u>but at the mouth of one witness he shall not be put to death</u>. The hands of the witnesses shall be first upon him to put him to death, and afterward the hands of all the people. So thou shalt put the evil away from among you (Deuteronomy 17:2-7).*

When the judges hear of wickedness they investigate the matter, and if they find the accusation to be true, then judgment is to be administered. There must be at least two witnesses that can truthfully verify the accusation. A single witness is not enough. Certain accusations may be brought to the pastor on an individual, but the pastor must confirm there is fault before he/she can do anything about it. The church court judges are not free to arbitrarily decide a judgment or punishment. They must do it by law.

If there arise a matter too hard for thee in judgment, between blood and blood, between plea and plea, and between stroke and stroke, being matters of controversy within thy gates: then shalt thou arise, and get thee up into the place which the LORD thy God shall choose; And thou shalt come unto the priests the Levites, and unto the judge that shall be in those days, and enquire; and they shall shew thee the sentence of judgment: And thou shalt do according to the sentence, which they of that place which the LORD shall choose shall shew thee; and thou shalt observe to do according to all that they inform thee: According to the sentence of the law which they shall teach thee, and according to the judgment which they shall tell thee, thou shalt do: thou shalt not decline from the sentence which they shall shew thee, to the right hand, nor to the left. And the man that will do presumptuously, and will not hearken unto the priest that standeth to minister there before the LORD thy God, or unto the judge, even that man shall die: and thou shalt put away the evil from Israel. And all the people shall hear, and fear, and do no more presumptuously (Deuteronomy 17:8-13).

Additional scriptural references:

- If sin is known, it is to be exposed before the authorities *(Leviticus 5:1)*.
- Do not conceal the behavior of the sinner *(Deuteronomy 13:6-8)*.
- Judge nothing before its time. There is a right time to judge *(Genesis 15:16; 1 Corinthians 4:5)*.
- The ministry must not be contentious, but instruct those who oppose themselves *(2 Timothy 2:24-26)*.

There are conditions where the church has no choice but to excommunicate some church members. An individual who fails to respect the judgment of the church is as one who elevates oneself ABOVE the church.

Backslider. The backslider is the individual that has ceased to live according to the Word of God or one who has sinned and has not repented of that sin. The backslider does not just suddenly "fall over the edge" into wrong or sin. Most of the time the backslider had already turned from God or overstepped His word in their heart long before evidence of wrongdoing was revealed. Iniquity begins in the heart with thoughts to do wrong! By ignoring the warnings of the Holy Ghost, the individual begins making plans to carry out his or her thoughts. For example, when one commits adultery, usually it is not a spur-of-the-moment thing but rather a premeditated act. Lust builds up in the heart and remains if unchallenged until the act is committed. *"If I regard iniquity in my heart, the LORD will not hear me" (Psalms 66:18)*. In the case of premeditated sin, there is generally an attempt to cover it up as King David did in his affair with Bathsheba. Ultimately, the heart is hardened by the deceitfulness of sin and, although the individual may remain in the congregation with the sin seemingly covered, the individual's heart has departed from God, and he or she has become a backslider in heart. *"<u>The backslider in heart shall be filled with his own ways</u>: and a good man shall be satisfied from himself" (Proverbs 14:14)*.

There are situations where one may be overtaken by temptation and fall into sin. In such case, the individual's heart is smitten with a transgression and will immediately seek to confess in order to be reconciled to God. Both the premeditated act and yielding to temptation are judged differently because the root cause is different. In the first case, the act was premeditated and presumptuous, operating from the self-will of the heart, whereas the latter was committed through weakness, carelessness or failing to take heed to counsel. Make no mistake: both were wrong. How the individuals respond to their wrongdoing is important if their recovery is to be achieved.

Unrepentant sin separates one from God. *"For, behold, the darkness shall cover the earth, and gross darkness the people: but the LORD shall arise upon thee, and his glory shall be seen upon thee" (Isaiah 60:2).* When one commits sin, the person's attitude toward the counsel of God, and the person's motives, will determine how recovery from the situation may take place (Jeremiah 5:25).

There are situations where there is a constant rejection of THE WORD of God, then that will put one beyond recovery. For instance, where King Saul "WOULD NOT" obey God's instruction (1 Samuel 15:9). Further, Samuel states to Saul *"thou has REJECTED THE WORD OF THE LORD and the Lord has rejected thee from being king over Israel"* (1 Samuel 15:26). Ultimately, the Lord told Samuel not to bother or pray for Saul because He had rejected him. *"And the LORD said unto Samuel, How long wilt thou mourn for Saul, seeing I have rejected him from reigning over Israel" (1 Samuel 16:1)?* There are conditions that put one beyond God's help, and it becomes futile to pray for that person. In the book of Jeremiah, there were three occasions where God told the prophet not to pray for the people for He would not hear or answer. *"Therefore pray not thou for this people, neither lift up a cry or prayer for them: for I will not hear them in the time that they cry unto me for their trouble" (Jeremiah 11:14).* Also see *(Jeremiah 7:16; Jeremiah 14:11-14; 1 John 5:16).*

When one has a self-willed and presumptuous attitude, and refuses to be instructed by the Word of God and/or the judicial process of the church, then that person is to be excommunicated or put out of fellowship with the church. Reconciliation is a complicated process.

Too often we try to bring the persons back into the congregation before God says otherwise. Until God gives the backslider a heart to repent, there is nothing the pastor can do to help. Church members may bring them into the pews, but not to God. When any church member feels he or she is greater than the church, by doing so any fellowship with God is immediately severed. *"They return, but not to the most High: they are like a deceitful bow: their princes shall fall by the sword for the rage of their tongue: this shall be their derision in the land of Egypt" (Hoses 7:16).* Often we coddle the backslider to entice him or her back into the church when the heart has not yet been changed. The danger is that we make these individuals to feel everything is all right simply because they have returned to take their place in the pew. God has a different opinion! *"Ephraim is joined to idols: let him alone" (Hosea 4:17).* LEAVE the individual ALONE. This is most difficult for many, but it is God's way until these individuals are willing to repent and turn from the presumptuousness of their ways. The presumptuous and self-willed spirits are the most difficult to deal with because they will not be instructed or recognize godly counsel. This is the root cause for the majority of backsliders, a cause that ultimately can lead to rejection by God and the torments of hell.

Note, the subsequent scriptural references on the dangers of a presumptuous spirit and a heart that is self-willed. If pastors fail to rid of the unclean thing from the congregation, it will eventually corrupt and destroy the whole congregation. A little leaven will contaminate the whole lump *(1 Corinthians 5:6).* *"Be not deceived: evil communications corrupt good manners" (1 Corinthians 15:33).*

- To be often reproved and harden the neck is to be destroyed without remedy *(Proverbs 29:1)*.
- The people transgressed – rejected the messenger – **no remedy** *(2 Chronicles 36:14-16)*.
- To turn the ear from hearing the law – prayers will not be heard *(Proverbs 28:9)*.
- Rebellion and stubbornness are sins that will cause one to be rejected *(1 Samuels 15:22-26)*.
- There is sin unto death – do not pray for it *(1 John 5:16)*.
- Those who do not obey the law are to be put out *(Ezra 7:26)*.
- The end of presumptuousness *(2 Peter 2:9-22)*.
- Esau despised his birthright and was rejected *(Hebrews 12: 15-17)*.

Unless God gives one a repentant heart, that person will not return. What should be our attitudes toward those who are backsliders or disfellowshipped? We are never justified, as children of God, to be rude, discourteous, uncivil or ungodly, toward those who have departed from the church. On the other hand, we must be firm in enforcing God's holy standards, showing love but never making backsliders feel comfortable in their state of wrong. Love is one thing, but fellowship back into the church is something else. Let God draw them to Him and prick their heart. When this happens, if their heart can be touched, they will repent, and all of heaven can rejoice over a lost soul recovered. If they refuse the overtures of God, there is no hope and all we may attempt to do will be of no avail. What good are our prayers if God will not hear them?

At no time should we rejoice over the flaws of wrongdoers nor hope for their destruction. Hell is a terrible place of unimaginable torment. Like heaven, it is eternal. We should hope for every lost soul to find repentance and recovery in the Kingdom of God.

The following scriptures describe God's attitude toward the backslider:

- They returned, but not to me. They returned to the church but not to God *(Hosea 7:16)*.
- Ephraim returned to Egypt (sin) and they eat the unclean thing *(Hosea 9:3)*.
- Mark them that cause offenses and avoid them *(Romans 16:17-18)*.
- Withdraw from the one who walks disorderly *(2 Thessalonians 3:14)*.
- Bid them, not God-speed who bring not the doctrine of truth *(2 John 1:9-12)*.
- Cast out the scorner and strife will cease *(Proverbs 22:10)*.
- Reject a heretic after the second admonition. They will subvert the soul *(Titus 3:10-11)*.
- Do not keep company with a transgressing brother nor have fellowship *(1 Corinthians 5:9-13)*.

7

Confession And Restoration

"He that covereth his sins shall not prosper: but whoso confesseth and forsaketh them shall have mercy. Happy is the man that feareth alway: but he that hardeneth his heart shall fall into mischief" (Proverbs 28:13-14).

Likewise, *"Brethren, if a man be overtaken in a fault, ye which are spiritual, restore such an one in the spirit of meekness; considering thyself, lest thou also be tempted" (Galatians 6:1).* None of us are so perfectly saved that it is impossible to fail or transgress the Word of God. This is not to say that one is destined to fall. Because God is more than able to keep us from falling (*Jude v. 24*), but the reality is that many fall through weakness or carelessness. God in His mercy has made provisions to reclaim those who have erred or transgressed in some manner. From the beginning of man's existence God has desired men to repent that He could restore them into fellowship with him. The record of God's attempt to get Cain to acknowledge his fault and offer the better sacrifice indicates His willingness to help man recover from his failure. Cain refused and instead of pleasing God, he murdered his brother Abel and was subsequently rejected by God. Confession and forsaking is God's way of getting man to acknowledge his sin and to be restored into His fellowship. As Cain lost out with God, so will we if we fail to recognize our wrong and do not change our conduct to please God.

"The Lord is not slack concerning his promise, as some men count slackness; but is longsuffering to us-ward, not willing that any should perish, but that all should come to repentance" (2 Peters 3:9). How then does the transgressor return to God? The obvious procedure is to repent, confess, and forsake accompanied by prayer by the pastor or one authorized by him. Is this all that is required? No! The ATTITUDE one has toward the transgression at hand, and the desire to be forgiven, are of the utmost importance. Attitude is one factor that is often eliminated from the restoration procedure. King David's attitude,

Have mercy upon me, O God, according to thy lovingkindness: according unto the multitude of thy tender mercies blot out my transgressions. Wash me throughly from mine iniquity, and cleanse me from my sin. For I acknowledge my transgressions: and my sin is ever before me. <u>Against thee, thee only, have I sinned, and done this evil in thy sight: that thou mightest be justified when thou</u>

speakest, and be clear when thou judgest (Psalms 51:1-4).

Often in confessing, there is not a sincere acknowledgment of one's sin, but there is an effort to justify what has been done to make the wrong appear less wrong.

What does it mean to confess? Confession is revealing a secret, making known the hidden thing. Confession is not simply admitting one has done wrong, but a willingness to purge one's self by vomiting out of their spiritual system the transgression. Confession is giving glory to God because He is righteous and we are sinfully wrong (*Psalms 51:1-4*). Being sorry for one's sin is not enough. There are many individuals who have shed tears and seemed sorry for their crime, not because they were truly sorry for their wrongdoing, but because they were caught. If one is to be reconciled to God, the person must be honest in the approach. God does not need to be informed that one has sinned. He already knows! *"O God, thou knowest my foolishness; and my sins are not hid from thee" (Psalms 69:5).*

Job learned that God knows all about us, and nothing is done in secret that He does not know nor see. He stated, *"For his eyes are upon the ways of man, and he seeth all his goings. There is no darkness, nor shadow of death, where the workers of iniquity may hide themselves" (Job 34:21-22).* These verses should make us aware that every action on our part is witnessed by God and it is incumbent upon man to acknowledge his transgression by willingly confessing so God might grant forgiveness and restore life to the soul. It is futile to hide one's wrong for even the darkness is as noonday to God. *"Woe unto them that seek deep to hide their counsel from the LORD, and their works are in the dark, and they say, Who seeth us? and who knoweth us" (Isaiah 29:15)*? The Gospel of Matthew states, everything will be revealed in time. *"Fear them not therefore: for there is nothing covered, that shall not be revealed; and hid, that shall not be known" (Matthew 10:26).* Only God is to be feared because He holds the key to life and death.

God is seeking genuine repentance, a complete change of heart, along with an acknowledgment of sin. The individual who sins is to confess to the authority of the church, the pastor. The pastor is the watchman of their souls and through prayer reconnects a broken relationship between the transgressor and God. Sin separates man from God and denies him any blessings from the Most High *(Isaiah 59:2; Jeremiah 5:25)*. Not only is separation a fact, but life is cut off and must be reestablished if the transgressor is to live. Transgressors will not confess until they are willing to see their transgression as vile and reprehensible before God, and are ready to repent. All God wants is for man to repent and confess he has sinned before God and be willing to acknowledge God's righteousness by his confession. God is more willing to forgive the transgressor than the transgressor is to receive His forgiveness. The rebellious spirit in man is so stubborn that the mere act of confession is so difficult to do. Man will do almost anything to avoid or circumvent it even at the expense of his soul. Only those who are genuinely interested in their soul will make right their wrongs so they can live and not die. For the transgressor, confession is the difference between life and death. *"If we confess our sins, he is faithful and just to forgive us our sins, and to cleanse us from all unrighteousness" (1 John 1:9).*

No one can restore themselves to God. As we are not able to preach the gospel to ourselves, or to baptize ourselves without the assistance of another person, neither can we plead our own case without the mediatory assistance of someone else.

Therefore if any man be in Christ, he is a new creature: old things are passed away; behold, all things are become new. And all things are of God, who hath reconciled us to himself by Jesus Christ, and hath given to us the ministry of reconciliation; To wit, that God was in Christ, reconciling the world unto himself, not imputing their trespasses unto them; and hath committed unto us the word of reconciliation (2 Corinthians 5:17-19).

The pastoral role is the mediator between man and God through Jesus Christ. The ministry of reconciliation is the link through preaching the gospel to the sinner and to aid the restoration of the transgressor. In the case of the transgressor, they need the help of one who has a connection with the Most High and can present their case to Him who has the power to forgive. Regarding restoration, the pastoral ministry has the authority to assist in reconnecting a broken fellowship by making an appeal to our Lord Jesus Christ, our chief advocate. *"My little children, these things write I unto you, that ye sin not. And if any man sin, we have an advocate with the Father, Jesus Christ the righteous" (1 John 2:1).* Note, "If any man" sin, this refers to the person who has sinned. "We have" is referring to the judicial authority of the church, the pastor with the deacons. The transgressor has a representative through the church ministry with Christ, who then pleads their case and provides forgiveness and restoration.

CONFESSION AND RESTORATION

And this is the confidence that we have in him, that, if we ask any thing according to his will, he heareth us: And if we know that he hear us, whatsoever we ask, we know that we have the petitions that we desired of him. If any man see his brother sin a sin which is not unto death, he shall ask, and he shall give him life for them that sin not unto death. There is a sin unto death: I do not say that he shall pray for it. All unrighteousness is sin: and there is a sin not unto death (1 John 5:14-17).

First, the church ministry has confidence in God that it will be heard in the petitions placed before him. This includes the appeal to restore the one who has sinned. In other words, God will honor the request. If any man sees his brother or sister sin a sin; who is the *any man*? This is the pastor of the local church. Next, how is it possible to *see* his brother sin? Was the pastor with the person when the person committed the sin? No! The pastor is not a police officer that follows the saints around and keeps a constant check on them. The word *see* means to come to the knowledge of a sin that has been committed. How is this knowledge acquired? By a confession on the part of the transgressor to the pastor. Now, the pastor must make a judgment decision. Is the sin a sin unto death or can there be life extended? It is necessary for the pastor to have a discerning spirit so that he can determine the nature and circumstances of the sin committed.

If the sin is not unto death, the pastor is to ask, that is, petition God through prayer on behalf of the guilty party. Remember, the pastor has confidence that God will hear his petition. As the pastor asks, then "he"; who is he? The "He" is God who will give "him", the pastor life for the person that sin not unto death. This is what happens. The pastor, after hearing the transgressor's confession, makes a petition unto God by praying for the person who has sinned. In return, God gives the pastor life through his prayer to restore into fellowship the one that has sinned. To be separated from the Church is to be separated from God and in order to be restored to life the individual must be brought back into fellowship with the church.

There is a sin unto death. What is it? It is the presumptuous, self-willed conduct of an individual who refuse to be instructed and is in total defiance of God's word and who against all advice to change, persists in doing their thing. The *"presumptuousness"* of sin is called the "great transgression" *(Psalms 19:13)*. During Jeremiah's time, Israel refused to hear the prophet and change her ways or turn from her sin. Three times God told Jeremiah not to pray for the people of Israel because He (God) would not hear the prophet's nor the people's prayer. Also, see *Jeremiah 7:16; 11:14.*

Then said the LORD unto me, <u>Pray not for this people for their good. When they fast, I will not hear their cry</u>; and when they offer burnt offering and an oblation, I will not accept them: but I will consume them by the sword, and by the famine, and by the pestilence. Then said I, Ah, Lord GOD! behold, the prophets say unto them, Ye shall not see the sword, neither shall ye have famine; but I will give you assured peace in this place. Then the LORD said unto me, The prophets prophesy lies in my name: I sent them not, neither have I commanded them, neither spake unto them: they prophesy unto you a false vision and divination, and a thing of nought, and the deceit *of their heart (Jeremiah 14:11-14).*

God gives a chance and opportunity for one to turn around and make right their wrong. However, after much pleading and counseling, if they still refuse to listen and persist in their self-will, there is no other choice but to cut them off. *"He, that being often reproved hardeneth his neck, shall suddenly be destroyed, and that without remedy" (Proverbs 29:1).* This applies equally to the sinner and transgressor in the church.

There are those who have sinned through ignorance. How do they know to confess? When they become aware of their actions being contrary to God's word, they have the obligation to confess.

Or if a soul swear, pronouncing with his lips to do evil, or to do good, whatsoever it be that a man shall pronounce with an oath, <u>and it be hid from him; when he knoweth of it, then he shall be guilty in one of these</u>. And it shall be, when he shall be guilty in one of these things, <u>that he shall confess that he hath sinned in that thing</u>: And he shall bring his trespass offering unto the LORD for his sin which he hath sinned, a female from the flock, a lamb or a kid of the goats, for a sin offering; and the priest shall make an atonement for him concerning his sin (Leviticus 5:4-6).

And the LORD spake unto Moses, saying, Speak unto the children of Israel, When a man or woman shall commit any sin that men commit, to do a trespass against the LORD, and that person be guilty; Then they shall confess their sin which they have done: and he shall recompense his trespass with the principal thereof, and add unto it the fifth part thereof, and give it unto him against whom he hath trespassed (Numbers 5:5-7).

When a confession is made, it must be open, voluntary, free, honest and sincere before it is acceptable. One cannot hide, evade, cover-up nor disguise the substance of their confession. Failing to confess, means that one remains out of fellowship with the church and is still guilty before God. They are without life. Confession is not a general statement that "I did wrong", but it must be specific that they did this or that and told in detail so all the guilt can be "vomited out" *(Leviticus 5:5-6).* The priest served as the intermediary between man and God in the Old Testament whereas, Jesus Christ is our advocate, and the pastoral ministry is the link between the transgressor and God in the New Testament Church.

Appropriate Attitude in Confession

The Prodigal Son.

And when he came to himself, he said, How many hired servants of my father's have bread enough and to spare, and I perish with hunger! I will arise and go to my father, and will say unto him, Father, I have sinned against heaven, and before thee, And am no more worthy to be called thy son: make me as one of thy hired servants. And he arose, and came to his father. But when he was yet a great way off, his father saw him, and had compassion, and ran, and fell on his neck, and kissed him. And the son said unto him, Father, I have sinned against heaven, and in thy sight, and am no more worthy to be called thy son (Luke 15:17-21).

The young man first came to himself. He said that his lifestyle did not bring any comfort or prosperity to his being or soul. Next, he determined to acknowledge his sin fully before his father. He makes no effort to blame anyone for his condition. "I did it on my own and am responsible for my situation," is essentially what his actions tell us. He states "I have sinned against heaven (God) and you. I am not worthy to be called your son. Just make me a servant." God will not bother anyone until they are ready to admit their sin. *"I will go and return to my place, till they acknowledge their offence, and seek my face: in their affliction they will seek me early" (Hosea 5:15).*

This is the same attitude that is to be demonstrated when one is confessing or is being restored back to the church. Many want to pick up where they left off, have their old office back, their place on the pulpit, etc. Their attitude should be, "I have disgraced the church and my God. Let me be restored into membership is all I am asking for. I make no excuse for my conduct and acknowledge my sin as reprehensible toward the church and God." Job puts it this way:

He looketh upon men, and if any say, I have sinned, and perverted that which was right, and it profited me not; He will deliver his soul from going into the pit, and his life shall see the light. Lo, all these things worketh God oftentimes with man, To bring back his soul from the pit, to be enlightened with the light of the living" (Job 33:27-30). Job's attitude changed when he saw his insignificance before God, *"Then Job answered the LORD, and said, Behold, I am vile; what shall I answer thee? I will lay mine hand upon my mouth. Once have I spoken; but I will not answer: yea, twice; but I will proceed no further (Job 40:3-5).* Also, see *Job 42:1-6.*

One of the best descriptions of confession and how it is to be carried out is found in the book of Joshua,

> *And Joshua said unto Achan, My son, give, I pray thee, glory to the LORD God of Israel, and make confession unto him; and tell me now what thou hast done; hide it not from me. And Achan answered Joshua, and said, Indeed I have sinned against the LORD God of Israel, and thus and thus have I done: When I saw among the spoils a goodly Babylonish garment, and two hundred shekels of silver, and a wedge of gold of fifty shekels weight, then I coveted them, and took them; and, behold, they are hid in the earth in the midst of my tent, and the silver under it (Joshua 7:19-21).*

We learn from this experience that sin can cause a disruption in the church. When this happens, it is the pastor's responsibility to seek out the cause as did Joshua. Sin is often behind confusion in the local church. When Achan was discovered, he was advised to give "glory to God." How? By confessing to Him. However, in confessing to God, the one who has sinned must tell "ME" (Joshua) what you have done and hide it not from ME. Note, in confessing to God, the guilty one confesses to a PERSON, the pastor. If we substitute the pastor for Joshua, we have the picture of the church; also, as stated before, the confession must be in detail. When Achan confessed, he said "I have sinned against God and *thus and thus* have I done." Even though some may question and disagree with this type of confession, it was nevertheless, God's way for Joshua and He is a God that does not change. What was good then in principle is still valid today. The following scripture references will add to the subject just discussed:

- If God's people will forsake and repent, He will come to

them *(Jeremiah 4:1)*.

- The Old Testament offering for sin *(Leviticus 4:27-30; 8:14-21)*.
- A little leaven (sin) can spoil the whole loaf *(1 Corinthians 5:1-6)*.
- I repent in dust and ashes *(Job 40:4; 42:5-6)*.
- David said, *"Against thee, thee only, have I sinned" (Psalms 51:1-4)*.
- When he came to himself – acknowledged that he sinned against heaven *(Luke 15:16-24)*.
- When sin is committed, confusion takes place *(Jeremiah 3:20-25)*.
- He that covers sin shall not prosper – confess and forsake *(Proverbs 28:13-14)*.
- Declare mine iniquity – be sorry for my sin *(Psalms 38:18)*.
- My iniquity is not hid (Psalms 32:5).
- When one has truly repented, there is absolute evidence of that repentance.

For godly sorrow worketh repentance to salvation not to be repented of: but the sorrow of the world worketh death. For behold this selfsame thing, that ye sorrowed after a godly sort, what carefulness it wrought in you, yea, what clearing of yourselves, yea, what indignation, yea, what fear, yea, what vehement desire, yea, what zeal, yea, what revenge! In all things ye have approved yourselves to be clear in this matter (2 Corinthians 7:10-11).

There are seven characteristics of repentance indicated in the above verse: *CAREFULNESS, CLEARING OF YOURSELF, INDIGNATION, WHAT FEAR, VEHEMENT DESIRE, ZEAL, and REVENGE.* These seven pieces of evidence of repentance are preceded by "godly sorrow". This sorrow is unlike the general thought of just being sorry for something, but sorrow that produces an intense grief that touches the very soul of the individual with a strong motivation to do something about it. It is a grief instilled by God's Spirit to make correction of the sin for which they have been guilty. The results of this grief are seen in the seven characteristics of repentance. Let us examine each of these seven characteristics:

1. *CAREFULNESS:* self-examination, earnestness for the purpose of avoiding the same condition, vigilance.
2. *CLEARING:* apologetic with remorse for their conduct, energetic to clear themselves of the stain by showing a disapproval of the attitude.
3. *INDIGNATION:* to detest and express a hatred for the evil (sin), angry over the deeds that were done.
4. *FEAR:* lest the person leave themselves unguarded again, and fall victim to the error of sin and the discipline that follows, alarm as the person recognizes the enormity of sinful conduct and its consequences.
5. *VEHEMENT DESIRE:* this longing for restored fellowship, a strong desire to please God in all things and to obtain His mercy and forgiveness for past errors and a refreshing of His Spirit.

CONFESSION AND RESTORATION

6. *ZEAL:* an intense desire to shun evil by cleaving to good; to employ the remedy for a godly life before God. A fervent motivation to do right. This zeal is expressed in actions and not words.
7. *REVENGE:* to be ruthless against all evil and to crush "wrong". To secure punishment against evildoers.

<u>These are the signs of a spiritual renewal and the evidence that true repentance has taken place.</u>

Pastoral Role in Confession

Only the pastor bears oversight in the confession process. The pastor may delegate the responsibility to another, but in the end, the pastoral role is held responsible. The pastor is the overseer *(Acts 20:28)* and the watchman for the soul *(Hebrews 13:17)*. *"Brethren, if a man be overtaken in a fault, ye which are spiritual, restore such an one in the spirit of meekness; considering thyself, lest thou also be tempted" (Galatians 6:1).* First, here is one that is overtaken by some sin and the individual fails to resist temptation through carelessness or weakness. "Ye which are spiritual" is referring to the ministry-- especially the pastor and not someone in the congregation who has given the impression that he or she is so spiritual and close to God. It is not the members' responsibility to restore anyone; this responsibility is the pastor's. There are those in every congregation who feel they have a special touch and understanding of people's problems and are inclined to make an effort to draw the unwary unto themselves.

The process here is not a "you have done wrong, now you have to pay" attitude, but one of gentleness and compassion to restore the person who has erred back to a place of right fellowship and service. This verse has the sense of an arm out of joint. Most of us know how painful this can be. The restoring is the effort to put this arm back in place. One would not be rough and unfeeling as he or she attempts to put it back into its socket. Instead, the person would use tenderness and gentleness to reduce the pain of the person affected. This is how the pastor is to treat the one overtaken in a fault. The one who is overtaken is grieved that he or she did such a thing, and our attitude is to help the person, not make the pain worse. Second, consider yourself lest you might need someone to help you. Would you want the same treatment as you dispensed to others? Think about it!

Is any sick among you? let him call for the elders of the church; and let them pray over him, anointing him with oil in the name of the Lord: And the prayer of faith shall save the sick, and the Lord shall raise him up; and if he have committed sins, they shall be forgiven him. Confess your faults one to another, and pray one for another, that ye may be healed. The effectual fervent prayer of a righteous man availeth much (James 5:14-16).

Some sicknesses are caused by sin. If the person is to recover, his sin must be purged. Call the elders (ministry) of the church and if person confesses his sin, the prayer of faith shall save the one who has sinned or who is ill as a result of such wickedness. How will the elders know if one has sinned unless it is confessed? Unfortunately, some have interpreted the latter part of the verse to mean a public confession. This is wrong and at no time is it in order to publicly (for individuals) make an open confession to the congregation for his or her misconduct. One might ask for forgiveness of one's conduct that is open to all, but a person should not confess personal sins openly. This is to be done before the pastor and his deacons. Neither does one confess to just anyone in the congregation. Some will endeavor to pick a friend and tell that friend of the wrongdoing, but the friend or whoever it may be is not qualified to receive this type of confession. This is a command between the individual saint and the pastor. Individual confessions are not made to open congregations, but in private before the proper church authorities. David acknowledges to Nathan, the seer, he was the guilty one, but he did not go before all Israel and declare his sin *(2 Samuel 12:1-14)*.

Acts 19:18-19, illustrates how all those who were in the church confessed their pagan practice by making a public confession of their transgression. They did so by building a huge fire in the city street and burned all their books on witchcraft thus letting everyone know that such practice was wrong and sinful. Only God can grant repentance to the transgressor; however, in His mercy He gives the erring one "space or time" to repent.

8

Tithes and Offerings

God has provided a means of financing His program since the beginning of time through voluntary giving (offerings) and the assessments called "tithes". Contrary to the opinion of many, tithes do not begin with the "Law", but was practiced by Abraham 430 years before the law *(Genesis 14:18-20)* and continued through Jacob *(Genesis 28:20-22)*, and finally through Levi (law) and the Levitical Priesthood. God employs the principle of "offerings" when He instructed Moses on how to acquire materials to build the tabernacle *(Exodus 25:1-8)* and later Solomon's Temple. The subject of "tithes & offerings" is widely practiced but often misunderstood as to its purpose and applications according to the scriptures. This portion of the study guide divides the subject matter of tithes and offerings into two distinct sections. The first section will deal with "TITHES," covering the definition and purpose according to Scripture. The second section will cover "OFFERINGS," and how they are used.

It is evident that one cannot pay tithes or give offerings unless there is some manner of INCOME" provided for the individual. This income may be money or wages, interest from investments, Social Security and welfare checks, bonuses, produce from the fields (farming), livestock (cattle, sheep, etc.), or anything that represents an increase to the individual. In biblical times tithes consisted of things harvested, increases in the flocks and herds, and money from the sale of produce as well as wages. Today, tithes and offerings are almost always paid in the currency of the time, and it is the exception to the rule to use commodities as the medium of exchange. As we begin, it is important to establish it is God who makes it possible for us to get wealth and is responsible for any increase one may enjoy. All that we possess in reality belongs to God, and He expects us to be faithful stewards over His things. The writer Moses stated,

And thou say in thine heart, My power and the might of mine hand hath gotten me this wealth. But thou shalt remember the LORD thy God: for it is he that giveth thee power to get wealth, that he may establish his covenant which he sware unto thy fathers, as it is this day (Deuteronomy 8:17-18).

Because of Him one has the strength, health, and opportunity to obtain and maintain employment. It is because of Him the fields and trees provide harvest and livestock reproduces to provide for us our needs.

In the final analysis, God owns everything, and all we are able to enjoy is on "loan from Him" that provides for our daily needs. *"The earth is the LORD'S, and the fulness thereof; the world, and they that dwell therein" (Psalms 24:1)*. Furthermore,

For every beast of the forest is mine, and the cattle upon a thousand hills. I know all the fowls of the mountains: and the wild beasts of the field are mine. If I were hungry, I would not tell thee: for the world is mine, and the fulness thereof (Psalms 50:10-12).

And finally,

Charge them that are rich in this world, that they be not highminded, nor trust in uncertain riches, but in the living God, who giveth us richly all things to enjoy; That they do good, that they be rich in good works, ready to distribute, willing to communicate; Laying up in store for themselves a good foundation against the time to come, that they may lay hold on eternal life (1Timothy 6:17-19).

God is the owner, controller, and generator of all that exists. These things are given to man for him to enjoy, but at the same time man has the obligation and responsibility to act as a good steward over God's abundant blessings. We are admonished not to put our trust in corruptible material things, for God can reclaim them as easy as He can provide them. He expects us to honor and give Him glory for the blessings we receive, and one way to do this is to honor Him with our tithes and offerings.

Tithes

Tithe is defined as the "tenth" or one tenth of one's total increase. The increase is defined as "the gross amount that is added to one's possessions". This is not limited to just gross wages, but any other increase that is added to your total resources, taxable or not. The writer Moses stated,

And all the tithe of the land, whether of the seed of the land, or of the fruit of the tree, is the LORD'S: it is holy unto the LORD. And if a man will at all redeem ought of his tithes, he shall add thereto the fifth part thereof. And concerning the tithe of the herd, or of the flock, even of whatsoever passeth under the rod, the tenth shall be holy unto the LORD (Leviticus 27:30-32).

Since the "tenth" belongs to God, He can dispose of it as He wishes. The "tenth" was given to the children of Levi for their service of the tabernacle. When one pays one's tithes, the money is no longer that person's, and he has no say so as to how it is to be used. It now belongs to God for Him to use and disburse. Perhaps the most familiar scripture on the subject of tithes,

Even from the days of your fathers ye are gone away from mine ordinances, and have not kept them. Return unto me, and I will return unto you, saith the LORD of hosts. But ye said, Wherein shall we return? Will a man rob God? Yet ye have robbed me. But ye say, Wherein have we robbed thee? In tithes and offerings. Ye are cursed with a curse: for ye have robbed me, even this whole nation. Bring ye all the tithes into the storehouse, that there may be meat in mine house, and prove me now herewith, saith the LORD of hosts, if I will not open you the windows of heaven, and pour you out a blessing, that there shall not be room enough to receive it. And I will rebuke the devourer for your sakes, and he shall not destroy the fruits of your ground; neither shall your vine cast her fruit before the time in the field, saith the LORD of hosts (Malachi 3:7-11).

Unfortunately, for some, this is the only scripture they know, but the purpose and procedure of dealing with tithes and offerings is unknown to them. Notice verse 7, God's indictment on his people, "you have gone away from mine ordinances and not kept them. Will a man rob God? How? In tithes and offerings". Note the distinction between tithes AND offerings: the robbery involved both. They once did tithe, but now they have slacked off and are no longer fulfilling their obligation to God. He calls them "robbers." Does one dare rob God? What is the nature of this robbery? They did not pay their tenth or give offerings and as a result, the House of God went lacking, and the priests were forced into the fields to work. The results, "you are cursed with a curse (v. 9). The Lord said bring ALL the tithes into the STOREHOUSE (church) that there may be meat in my house – if you will, I will pour out a blessing more than you can contain (v. 10). Paying tithes and giving offerings bring a blessing of a magnitude that there will be insufficient room to receive it; however, failing to pay tithes bring on the individual a "curse", God's disfavor in all their activities.

Please note that tithes are a DEBT one OWES to God. It is a fixed percentage of one's total increase. On the other hand, an offering is the amount the individual chooses to give as a voluntary gift. One does not GIVE one's tithes. Do you "give" the bank your mortgage loan payment or do you PAY your loan to the bank? The mortgage money does not belong to the borrower, it is a loan and a debt. The motgagee is expected to return that money with interest by PAYING on the debt at an agreed upon rate. SINCE TITHES ARE A DEBT, WE PAY TITHES, BUT WE GIVE OFFERINGS. When one fails to pay tithes, that person is stealing from God. The nine-tenths God allows us to keep, coupled with His blessings, is far better than keeping it all for ourselves.

The eighth commandment reads, *"Thou shalt not steal" (Exodus 20:15).* Since the tithes belong to God, doesn't this commandment also apply to the things belonging to Him? Is robbing God any less a sin because it is God's stuff? NO! It is a dangerous thing to rob God. The first fruits belong to God, and when we receive our increase, our obligation is to give God that which belongs to Him FIRST. First fruits are the gross amount of the paycheck; it is the first thing paid from the paycheck before the house note, car payment, grocery bill, and credit card, and etc. The IRS does not trust us to pay our taxes, so they take their portion first to make sure they get it. Most never see the amount of deduction taken from their check. It is just a number. However, God is entitled to the first payment before anything else is paid and trusts the individual to pay on time. *"Honour the LORD with thy substance, and with the firstfruits of all thine increase: So shall thy barns be filled with plenty, and thy presses shall burst out with new wine" (Proverbs 3:9-10).*

It Takes Faith To Give God The "Tenth" With A Willing Heart. God set the principle of tithes in the garden when He reserved a portion for Himself and not for Adam or Eve; the tree of the *"knowledge of good and evil" (Genesis 2:17).* They were not to eat of this tree and to do so would result in the penalty of death. It was reserved for God and God alone. As a result of partaking of this tree, man received a death sentence and a curse was placed upon the earth. Compare the principle with *Malachi 3:9*, where a curse is pronounced for robbing God of the tithes. The purpose of tithes was to ensure *"Meat in mine house" (Malachi 3:10)*. This is in reference to the Word & Truth dispensed by the ministry. This was God's financial way of compensating the Levitical Priests and the Ministry of today for their services for Him. *"Who then is a faithful and wise servant, whom his lord hath made ruler over his household, to give them meat in due season" (Matthew 24:45)?* The reference here is the responsibility of the ministry to feed the flock of God with the Word.

While details of tithing are outlined in the Old Testament, not too much is stated in the New Testament. However, there are enough distinct references made in the New Testament to give authority for the ministry to collect the tithe from the children of God. Consider the Apostles, who were Jews, and well acquainted with the Old Testament system of tithing. They saw no problem in applying the same system to the church. Jesus justifies paying tithes, accusing the Pharisees and hypocrites, who paid tithes of aromatic spice and herbs, of having left off the weightier matters of the law, judgment, mercy, and faith *(Matthew 23:23)*. These (tithing) they were to do AND NOT LEAVE THE OTHER UNDONE. Note the following scriptures:

- *"If ye be Christ's then ye are Abraham's seed" (Galatians 3:29).*
- If we are Abraham's children then we are to do the works

of Abraham, that is, pay tithes as Abraham did *(John 8:39)*.

- Abraham gave tithes of ALL to Melchizedek, God Himself *(Genesis 14:18-20)*.
- Jacob vowed a vow that included giving a "tenth" unto God *(Genesis 28:20-22)*.

The writer Moses stated,

And the LORD spake unto Aaron, Thou shalt have no inheritance in their land, neither shalt thou have any part among them: I am thy part and thine inheritance among the children of Israel. And, behold, I have given the children of Levi all the tenth in Israel for an inheritance, for their service which they serve, even the service of the tabernacle of the congregation (Numbers 18:20-21).

If something is mine, then I have the right to dispose of it as I see fit. Since the tenth or tithes belong to God, He has the right to dispose of it as He sees fit. He gives it to the church to perpetuate the work of the ministry.

- Moses gave you circumcision not because it was of Moses, but of the fathers *(John 7:22)*. Both circumcision AND tithing came from Abraham.
- The Levites were to TAKE tithes of the children of Israel *(Numbers 18:26)*.

Note the following scriptural reference and the present verb tenses in the statement.

And verily they that are of the sons of Levi, who receive the office of the priesthood, have a commandment to take tithes of the people according to the law, that is, of their brethren, though they come out of the loins of Abraham: But he whose descent is not counted from them received tithes of Abraham, and blessed him that had the promises. And without all contradiction the less is blessed of the better. And here men that die receive tithes; but there he receiveth them, of whom it is witnessed that he liveth. And as I may so say, Levi also, who receiveth tithes, payed tithes in Abraham. For he was yet in the loins of his father, when Melchisedec met him. (Hebrews 7:5-10).

They that *ARE* the *"SONS OF LEVI"* (*Malachi 3:10*) who *RECEIVE* the office of the priesthood *HAVE* a *COMMANDMENT TO TAKE TITHES* of the people according to the law or system. Note, the use of the present tense in the above verse. Please note four things:

1. The ministry is now in the place of the Priesthood, who *are the sons of Levi.*

2. The ministry is now instructed to *"take tithes* of the people."

3. Tithes are to be taken *"according to the law"* (system).

4. The ministry, which takes tithes, also *PAYS tithes.*

Furthermore, *"And the priest the son of Aaron shall be with the Levites, when the Levites take tithes: and the Levites shall bring up the tithe of the tithes unto the house of our God, to the chambers, into the treasure house" (Nehemiah 10:38).* Tithes are brought to the church and not sent to the foreign field, sent to support a TV broadcast, given to the poor, or distributed as the individual chooses. The church is the "storehouse" or "treasure house" and it is the responsibility of the pastor to disburse for the use of the ministry as he is directed by God.

The Levites were to offer a "heave offering" consisting of a tenth part of the tithe. This tithe of the tithe was to be given to Aaron and included gifts they received. The tithe of the people was given to the Levites as their inheritance *(Numbers 18:24)*. They were to tithe the tithe as it was their income, the equivalent to the people's increase *(Numbers 18:26-31)*. To deny or restrict the ministry of their income is wrong. Jealousy, envy, resentment are often the root causes behind such restrictions.

Do ye not know that they which minister about holy things live of the things of the temple? and they which wait at the altar are partakers with the altar? Even so hath the Lord ordained that they which preach the gospel should live of the gospel (1 Corinthians 9:13-14).

If paying tithes and giving offerings was not required in the New Testament Church then where did the material substance (money) come from that provided a living for the preachers of the gospel? The ministry is to live of the things of the temple (church), and they that are ordained to preach the gospel should live of the gospel indicating some form of systematized income (the tithing system). Also see *Luke 18:12* and *Nehemiah 13:10-12*. These principles were established BEFORE the law, DURING the law, and AFTER the law. Under the law the use of tithes was for those who did the service (Levites and Priests) of the tabernacle or temple; however, now the use of the tithe is for the ministry of the church.

Law of Tithes

The Book of Leviticus states,

And all the tithe of the land, whether of the seed of the land, or of the fruit of the tree, is the LORD'S: it is holy unto the LORD. And if a man will at all redeem ought of his tithes, he shall add thereto the fifth part thereof. And concerning the tithe of the herd, or of the flock, even of whatsoever passeth under the rod, the tenth shall be holy unto the LORD (Leviticus 27:30-32).

This passage states ALL the tithes belong to the Lord. The tithe is paid to God, not the pastor. The pastor gets the use of it, but the payment is made unto God for his service. The tithe is to be paid at the place God chooses (storehouse - church) and not where one wishes to choose.

But unto the place which the LORD your God shall choose out of all your tribes to put his name there, even unto his habitation shall ye seek, and thither thou shalt come: And thither ye shall bring your burnt offerings, and your sacrifices, and your tithes, and heave offerings of your hand, and your vows, and your freewill offerings, and the firstlings of your herds and of your flocks: And there ye shall eat before the LORD your God, and ye shall rejoice in all that ye put your hand unto, ye and your households, wherein the LORD thy God hath blessed thee. Ye shall not do after all the things that we do here this day, every man whatsoever is right in his own eyes (Deuteronomy 12:5-8).

Currently, the place one's tithe is paid is the local church where individuals place their membership. See *Deuteronomy 12:5-8; 10-14*. In Moses's writing,

TITHES AND OFFERINGS

And, behold, I have given the children of Levi all the tenth in Israel for an inheritance, for their service which they serve, even the service of the tabernacle of the congregation. Neither must the children of Israel henceforth come nigh the tabernacle of the congregation, lest they bear sin, and die. But the Levites shall do the service of the tabernacle of the congregation, and they shall bear their iniquity: it shall be a statute forever throughout your generations, that among the children of Israel they have no inheritance. But the tithes of the children of Israel, which they offer as an heave offering unto the LORD, I have given to the Levites to inherit: therefore I have said unto them, Among the children of Israel they shall have no inheritance. And the LORD spake unto Moses, saying, Thus speak unto the Levites, and say unto them, When ye take of the children of Israel the tithes which I have given you from them for your inheritance, then ye shall offer up an heave offering of it for the LORD, even a tenth part of the tithe. And this your heave offering shall be reckoned unto you, as though it were the corn of the threshingfloor, and as the fulness of the winepress. Thus ye also shall offer an heave offering unto the LORD of all your tithes, which ye receive of the children of Israel; and ye shall give thereof the LORD'S heave offering to Aaron the priest. Out of all your gifts ye shall offer every heave offering of the LORD, of all the best thereof, even the hallowed part thereof out of it. Therefore thou shalt say unto them, When ye have heaved the best thereof from it, then it shall be counted unto the Levites as the increase of the threshingfloor, and as the increase of the winepress. And ye shall eat it in every place, ye and your households: for it is your reward for your service in the tabernacle of the congregation (Numbers 18:21-31).

In these verses, God gives the "tenth" to the Levites (the ministry) and gives instructions how it is to be used and the freedom of its use. This is their paycheck for the service in the tabernacle. Additionally, see *Numbers 18:26-31*. Furthermore, in the Apostle Paul's writing,

Say I these things as a man? or saith not the law the same also? For it is written in the law of Moses, Thou shalt not muzzle the mouth of the ox that treadeth out the corn. Doth God take care for oxen? Or saith he it altogether for our sakes? For our sakes, no doubt, this is written: that he that ploweth should plow in hope; and that he that thresheth in hope should be partaker of his hope. If we have sown unto you spiritual things, is it a great thing if we shall reap your carnal things? (1 Corinthians 9:8-11).

If we sow spiritual things, it is not unreasonable to reap material things. The saints are not to muzzle the mouth of the ox that treads out the corn; meaning, the pastor and the ministry are not to be denied that which they are rightly due. God will take good care of those who serve at His pleasure. Remember, God is the pastor's paymaster and He will not defraud anyone who has been commissioned by Him to do service for the people of God. Even if there is a shortage of tithes because people fail to pay, God is still obligated to take care of His own "employees". There is, however, one restriction. When God promises to take care of His servants, He does not intend for them to be excessive or wasteful of the blessings the servant receives. The pastor must always remember that he or she is the steward of God's substance and is not to become greedy for filthy lucre or to strive to follow the trends and fashions of the world. As written,

> *Thou shalt truly tithe all the increase of thy seed, that the field bringeth forth year by year. And thou shalt eat before the LORD thy God, in the place which he shall choose to place his name there, the tithe of thy corn, of thy wine, and of thine oil, and the firstlings of thy herds and of thy flocks; that thou mayest learn to fear the LORD thy God always" (Deuteronomy 14:22-23).*

The individuals who truly pay tithes do not withhold back but consider all their increase in whatever form when paying tithes. Tithes are paid on the gross earnings and any other kind of increase.

> *"Thou shalt not delay to offer the first of thy ripe fruits, and of thy liquors: the firstborn of thy sons shalt thou give unto me. Likewise shalt thou do with thine oxen, and with thy sheep: seven days it shall be with his dam; on the eighth day thou shalt give it me (Exodus 22:29-30).*

One of the problems in paying tithes is when one delays or defers to pay. God requires one to pay on time. To delay is to add a double burden the next time and often, one becomes so far behind that he fails to pay altogether. It is far better to pay one's tithes as the income is received without delay. There have been cases where individuals fall so far behind in paying their tithes and allowed the devil to discourage them into thinking there was no use to continue serving God, and ultimately has backslidden from the church. Satan works on a believer's guilty conscience and will use any and every ploy to recapture those who have once been delivered from his hand.

In *Nehemiah 13:5, 10-12*, the Levites had to return to the fields because the people failed to pay their tithes. This is the same as forcing the pastor to return to his secular job to support his family because the church members fail to pay their tithes as they should. Many disgruntled church members have tried to use this tactic, failing to pay their tithes, to force a pastor to leave the church so they could get one to their own liking. If the pastor is really God's person, he will stick it out, and God will prove deliverance.

- The ministry is "encouraged" because the people paid their tithes *(2 Chronicles 31:4-10)*.
- By paying tithes the ministry will "cause" a blessing on your house (Ezekiel 44:30).
- When the Levites and priests received their tithes, the people rejoiced for them *(Nehemiah 12:44)*.
- We are to "esteem" the ministry highly *(1 Thessalonians 5:12-13)*.

When the total tithes have been given, the people were to testify or acknowledge that all had been paid. In other words, they had to provide a record of the tithe paid. Today this is through our method of tithe envelopes. It is a necessity in today's time to keep accurate records of membership donations for tax purposes and to justify church income and expenditures in the event of potential government inspection of church finances. It is the responsibility of the ministry to teach the people to tithe and if the ministry fails, it will be called into question.

TITHES AND OFFERINGS

The ministry or pastor is to pay tithes as others. The tithes are offered to the church treasury as part of the pastor's obligation to the "service of the sanctuary". Levi received tithes and he paid tithes as well. The Levites were required to "charge themselves" to give a certain amount for the "service of the sanctuary" *(Nehemiah 10:32-39; Numbers 18:26)*. This is the modern day authority for pledging to help carry the burden of the needs of the church.

Aaron was given the responsibility of managing the money that came to the temple because of the "anointing" that rested on him. The managing of the church finances is the responsibility of the pastor by the reason of the "anointing" invested in him or her. The pastor may delegate the work to others, but it is the pastor's responsibility to oversee the affairs of the church.

"And the LORD spake unto Aaron, Behold, I also have given thee the charge of mine heave offerings of all the hallowed things of the children of Israel; unto thee have I given them by reason of the anointing, and to thy sons, by an ordinance forever" (Numbers 18:8).

Pastors, beware not to be guilty of being greedy for "filthy lucre" and using all the tithes for yourselves. Tithes are for the MINISTRY. They are to be utilized to assist the ministry in the local church and for the ministry in smaller churches as well. While it is true that smaller churches must use the majority of the tithe to support the pastor; however, such a pastor must learn to live within his or her means and not try to compete with the personnel of larger congregations with luxury cars, big homes, etc. Remember, the tithe of the tithes belongs to the church treasury.

Offerings

When considering the subject of tithes and offerings often the emphasis is placed only on the tithes and rarely on the OFFERINGS. The charge is that the people have robbed God of tithes and OFFERINGS *(Malachi 3:7-11)*. Tithes were used principally for the Priest and Levites, which are the equivalent of today's ministry. Offerings are used to support the house of God, to supply the maintenance and other needs of the church building, utilities, service requirements, etc. While we speak of a free will offering as a general offering for the church, there may be a number of special offerings for specific needs as well as pledges to offset significant costs of purchase and repairs.

Offerings are given according to the measure of God's blessing of an individual and are not a fixed percentage of the "one tenth" or tithe. In fact, offerings could well be MORE than tithes in some cases. God placed on Aaron the responsibility of overseeing the money because of the anointing resting on him as the High Priest. The pastor has that same anointing and responsibility (Numbers 18:8). The pastor is held accountable by God to use wisely the assets of the church treasury and is not to be foolish or wasteful just because there is money to be used. God's house deserves the best, but it requires one who is prudent and skilled in managing those assets. Because God has called and ordained the pastor to be an overseer, He is holding the pastor responsible for the entire business transactions of the church. The anointing rests upon the pastor by the office he or she holds and not because of the person. It is needful in most cases to have a staff that can assist in church management to relieve the pastor of more spiritual duties, but the responsibility still belongs to the pastor.

"Honour the LORD with thy substance, and with the firstfruits of all thine increase: So shall thy barns be filled with plenty, and thy presses shall burst out with new wine" (Proverbs 3:9-10). These verses speak of three things: honor, substance, and firstfruits. To honor or give glory to God is to OBEY His commands. In this verse, honoring God is through giving offerings and paying tithes. The substance is that part of our increase that remains after the tithes have been paid. It is from the substance that offerings of various descriptions are given. Substance belongs to the individual for his or her use as seen fit. First fruit is the tithe. If one will be faithful in paying one's tithes and generous in giving of offerings, God promised that the person would be blessed in having the things that will make the person "full" and "happy." Note the following scripture: *"Give unto the LORD the glory due unto his name: bring an offering, and come into his courts" (Psalms 96:8).*

Moses was commissioned by God to build a "Sanctuary for Him". This required building materials of all kinds along with gold, silver, brass, etc. Also precious jewels and fine linen were required to fulfill the vision of God's sanctuary shown to Moses on Mount Sinai. Before he could begin, Moses had to ask the people for offerings of all the things required to build the Sanctuary as directed. This material came from Egypt and was carried by the people into the wilderness. Now God was to put all these things to use and commands Moses to:

Speak unto the children of Israel, that they bring me an offering: of every man that giveth it willingly with his heart ye shall take my offering. And this is the offering which ye shall take of them; gold, and silver, and brass, And blue, and purple, and scarlet, and fine linen, and goats' hair, And rams' skins dyed red, and badgers' skins, and shittim wood, Oil for the light, spices for anointing oil, and for sweet incense, Onyx stones, and stones to be set in the ephod, and in the breastplate. And let them make me a sanctuary; that I may dwell among them (Exodus 25:2-8).

How was Moses to acquire these things? By asking the people to bring them with a willing heart. This should be an answer to the critics who complain that "all the church does is ask for money." Notice it was God, who in the beginning of constructing a structure for worship, asked for a free-will offering from the congregation. Subsequently, Ezra was given a similar command when the temple was in the process of being built.

Thus saith Cyrus king of Persia, The LORD God of heaven hath given me all the kingdoms of the earth; and he hath charged me to build him an house at Jerusalem, which is in Judah. Who is there among you of all his people? his God be with him, and let him go up to Jerusalem, which is in Judah, and build the house of the LORD God of Israel, (he is the God,) which is in Jerusalem. And whosoever remaineth in any place where he sojourneth, let the men of his place help him with silver, and with gold, and with goods, and with beasts, beside the freewill offering for the house of God that is in Jerusalem (Ezra 1:2-4).

The offering was to be brought to Ezra BESIDE THE FREEWILL OFFERING FOR THE HOUSE OF GOD. The offering that we give to the church is of an amount we choose to give; however, the special offering is provided in ADDITION to our regular church offerings. One should not divide up the original offering into little pieces, but it is kept whole. To pledge into the building fund, for example, is not at the expense of one's regular offering, but an amount in addition to one's regular offering. The following verses are examples of the special offerings that were asked for,

These are the feasts of the LORD, which ye shall proclaim to be holy convocations, to offer an offering made by fire unto the LORD, a burnt offering, and a meat offering, a sacrifice, and drink offerings, every thing upon his day: Beside the sabbaths of the LORD, and beside your gifts, and beside all your vows, and beside all your freewill offerings, which ye give unto the LORD (Leviticus 23:37-38). "And they received from Moses all the offerings, which the children of Israel had brought for the work of the service of the sanctuary to make it withal. And they brought yet unto him free offerings every morning (Exodus 36:3).

Freewill offerings are regular offerings dedicated for the maintenance and supply of God's house.

And thou shalt keep the feast of weeks unto the LORD thy God with a tribute of a freewill offering of thine hand, which thou shalt give unto the LORD thy God, according as the LORD thy God hath blessed thee: Every man shall give as he is able, according to the blessing of the LORD thy God which he hath given thee (Deuteronomy 16:10, 17).

Moreover,

Now therefore perform the doing of it; that as there was a readiness

to will, so there may be a performance also out of that which ye have. For if there be first a willing mind, it is accepted according to that a man hath, and not according to that he hath not (2 Corinthians 8:11-12).

Another scriptural reference on the subject,

When thou shalt vow a vow unto the LORD thy God, thou shalt not slack to pay it: for the LORD thy God will surely require it of thee; and it would be sin in thee. But if thou shalt forbear to vow, it shall be no sin in thee. That which is gone out of thy lips thou shalt keep and perform; even a freewill offering, according as thou hast vowed unto the LORD thy God, which thou hast promised with thy mouth (Deuteronomy 23:21-23).

Scripture offers insight on "freewill offerings" and the attitude by which they are to be offered. It is giving as God has blessed and to give according to one's ability. One should give with a willing mind and to not allow emotions to govern the giving process. Therefore, if you don't have it don't promise it, and if you make a promise to give (pledge), then pay what you have vowed. *"Be not rash with thy mouth, and let not thine heart be hasty to utter any thing before God: for God is in heaven, and thou upon earth: therefore let thy words be few" (Ecclesiastes 5:2).* This verse warns against being overtaken by emotions and promising more than one can deliver. When the church is seeking pledges be generous but be sensible. Pledge within your ability for God will hold everyone accountable for his or her failed promises.

And Jehoash said to the priests, All the money of the dedicated things that is brought into the house of the LORD, even the money of every one that passeth the account, the money that every man is set at, and all the money that cometh into any man's heart to bring into the house of the LORD, Let the priests take it to them, every man of his acquaintance: and let them repair the breaches of the house, wheresoever any breach shall be found (2 Kings 12:4-5).

These particular verses dealt with a repair problem and each one set for him a certain amount toward repairing the house of God. This is the same as making a pledge.

Also we made ordinances for us, to charge ourselves yearly with the third part of a shekel for the service of the house of our God; For the shewbread, and for the continual meat offering, and for the continual burnt offering, of the sabbaths, of the new moons, for the set feasts, and for the holy things, and for the sin offerings to make an atonement for Israel, and for all the work of the house of our God (Nehemiah 10:32-33).

In addition to the previous verse, the Levites were to charge themselves--or using the parlance of today, they were to "pledge"--to give a certain amount of their "income" to provide for the necessary items used in the temple worship. For a pastor to think that he or she is exempt from this kind of giving is mistaken—the pastor is under the same obligation that the people must live by. *"And thou shalt take the atonement money of the children of Israel, and shalt appoint it for the service of the tabernacle of the congregation; that it may be a memorial unto the children of Israel before the LORD, to make an atonement for your souls" (Exodus 30:16).* There are special offerings taken for specific purposes and they must be used to that effect.

And it came to pass after this, that Joash was minded to repair the house of the LORD. And he gathered together the priests and the Levites, and said to them, Go out unto the cities of Judah, and gather of all Israel money to repair the house of your God from year to year, and see that ye hasten the matter. Howbeit the Levites hastened it not. And the king called for Jehoiada the chief, and said unto him, Why hast thou not required of the Levites to bring in out of Judah and out of Jerusalem the collection, according to the commandment of Moses the servant of the LORD, and of the congregation of Israel, for the tabernacle of witness? (2 Chronicles 24:4-6)

Those who are assigned to do the work or service in the House of God must give an accounting of the finances they receive to do the work. If they fail, they will be called into question and action will be taken against them. Dilatory attitudes should not be tolerated in the management of God's church.

When we give unto the Lord or make a vow to offer something to the church, it should involve some sacrifice on our part. David, when he wanted to build an altar to offer sacrifices to God, he was offered the threshing floor of Araunah's as a gift. But David refused to accept it because it did not cost him anything. *"And the king said unto Araunah, Nay; but I will surely buy it of thee at a price: neither will I offer burnt offerings unto the LORD my God of that which doth cost me nothing. So David bought the threshingfloor and the oxen for fifty shekels of silver"* *(2 Samuel 24:24).* This should be a lesson for us in determining the generosity of our offerings to the church. There should be some "sacrifice" when one gives. It is not always how much (quantity) one gives, but the motive and attitude behind the giving. Jesus points out the widow who gave the two mites, all that she had, which in God's sight was more than the abundance of the rich. As a rule, those with less often give more proportionally than those who have much.

And Jesus sat over against the treasury, and beheld how the people cast money into the treasury: and many that were rich cast in much. And there came a certain poor widow, and she threw in two mites, which make a farthing. And he called unto him his disciples, and saith unto them, Verily I say unto you, That this poor widow hath cast more in, than all they which have cast into the treasury: For all they did cast in of their abundance; but she of her want did cast in all that she had, even all her living (Mark 12:41-44).

God loves the cheerful giver and is adverse to the stingy one who is tight with his or her substance. If one does not sow many seeds, then that person will not reap a bountiful harvest. Little giving, little received.

But this I say, He which soweth sparingly shall reap also sparingly; and he which soweth bountifully shall reap also bountifully. Every man according as he purposeth in his heart, so let him give; not grudgingly, or of necessity: for God loveth a cheerful giver. And God is able to make all grace abound toward you; that ye, always having all sufficiency in all things, may abound to every good work (2 Corinthians 9:6-8).

The other offerings we give are not to be given at the expense of

our regular church offering. The following scriptural references illustrate the blessings of liberality. "The liberal soul shall be made fat: and he that watereth shall be watered also himself" (Proverbs 11:25). Moreover, "Give, and it shall be given unto you; good measure, pressed down, and shaken together, and running over, shall men give into your bosom. For with the same measure that ye mete withal it shall be measured to you again" (Luke 6:38). Paul, knowing that there were some deficiencies in Jerusalem where the church was in dire need, organized an offering to be taken on a regular basis and set aside for the need of the church at an appointed time. This illustrates the need for some sort of organized giving for the poor and other localities in need. During the time of national disaster, for instance, churches have collected monies to help alleviate the suffering of those in these disasters. Perhaps the best example of this special organized collection is the Foreign Missions Offering collected by churches in the Pentecostal Assemblies of the World each second Sunday of the month for the International Missions Department. "Now concerning the collection for the saints, as I have given order to the churches of Galatia, even so do ye" (1 Corinthians 16:1).

The Heave Offerings. It is a gift to God. Those offerings which the children of Israel voluntarily gave or were prescribed by the law. These offerings were separated from what the priests presented to God; not as a sacrifice, but as an offering.

Afterword

The principles of this book have been applied in the church where the author pastored consisted of a small congregation. The principles were instrumental on establishing the leadership of the church and directing the vision of the ministry. Every need of the ministry was met and the church is deb free along with many major improvements. The ministry has fulfilled all its organizational requirements completely and has been able to assist other churches as well as helping other pastors in need. As pastor, the author's personal needs have been satisfied without the support of a pastoral benefits package or an outside job. Fundraising efforts such as church dinners, bingo games, or any other special way to acquire finance have not been necessary to support the ministry. Tithes and offerings are the only sources of income of our church and God has blessed in a tremendous way because the people have been taught and

AFTERWORD

have obeyed; hence, they are blessed. When the people are blessed, the church will be blessed.

Author

Dr. Harry L. Herman was born in Indianapolis, Indiana, Nov. 14, 1924, where he was baptized in Jesus name and filled with the Holy Ghost on July 5th, 1949. He grew up in the mother church, Christ Temple. He served in the U.S. army in the pacific theatre in World War II.

On October 9, 1949 he married Jenny Rea "Jerry" Herman, and the Lord blessed them with 5 sons. Bishop Herman and Dr. "Jerry" were active members of Christ Temple. He served in almost every department of the church, and in 1960-1965 he served as Assistant Pastor, being called to Christ Temple in Detroit to pastor. He received his fellowship Certificate for the ministry in March 1955 with the A.B.S.A. He became the chairman of the Sunday School Department and the assistant chairman of the Young People's Department in the A.B.S.A.

AUTHOR

He was elevated to the Bishopric in the Pentecostal Assemblies of the World, Inc. in March 1989 and consecrated in August 1989. He is a member of the Executive Bishop's Council, and an active member of the Board of Bishops. He has served on many committees; the Pulpit Committee, License & Credential Committee, Chairman and member of the Judicial Committee, and Director of the I.C.E.A. He is a well-known Bible teacher who stands firmly on the Apostolic Doctrine. He receive his early teaching from his parents, who received their teaching from the late Bishop G. T. Haywood, and Elder Robert F. Tobin. His ministry was further enhanced by reading Bishop Haywood's writings and sitting under the late Bishop Morris E. Golder, and the late Bishop Willie Lee. He served as Diocesan of the Minnesota, Wisconsin, & Dakotas Council for 6 1/2 years before being appointed Diocesan of the Northern District Council March (Michigan) from 1996-2013. He was elected Chairman of the Council in 1984 for two terms and served as District Elder for 11 years.

He moved his family to Kalamazoo at the invitation of the late Bishop Ross P. Paddock in September 1970 to become the Assistant Pastor of Christ Temple Kalamazoo. Bishop Paddock resigned June 5, 1972 as Pastor and Bishop Herman was elected the Pastor, faithfully serving until January 31, 2010. He has a perfect record in Sunday School for 34 years as a teacher. He received an honorary Doctor of Divinity from the Aenon Bible College in 1994, and earned a Doctor of Theology and a Doctor of Divinity in 1995 from the International Apostolic College. He is an esteemed counselor and teacher of young ministers, pastors, and married couples.

www.ingramcontent.com/pod-product-compliance
Lightning Source LLC
LaVergne TN
LVHW011210080426
835508LV00007B/713